NOW

First published by O-Books, 2011
O-Books is an imprint of John Hunt Publishing Ltd.,
Laurel House, Station Approach, Alresford, Hants, SO24 9JH, UK
office1@o-books.net
www.o-books.com

For distributor details and how to order please visit the 'Ordering' section on our website.

Text copyright: Richard Singer 2010

ISBN: 978 1 84694 524 3

A CIP catalogue record for this book is available from the British Library.

Design: David Kerby

Printed in the United States of America

We operate a distinctive and ethical publishing philosophy in all
areas of our business, from our global network of authors to
production and worldwide distribution.

NOW
Embracing the Present Moment

Richard A. Singer Jr.

Award Winning Author of
Your Daily Walk with the Great Minds

BOOKS

Winchester, UK
Washington, USA

Praise for *Now*

"Richard Singer's new book NOW is filled with quotes from great teachers throughout the ages, and the guidance to help you build your own practice of daily mindfulness. Beautiful!"
Lissa Coffey
Best Selling Author, CLOSURE and the Law of Relationship

"This gem of a book brings together the wisdom of poets, preachers, prophets and pilgrims, always taking us on the right direction on the lonely way back home, to the present moment, this wonderful moment. Please savor every line of wisdom this book provides."
David J. Powell, Ph.D.
President, International Center for Health Concerns, Inc.

"Richard A. Singer, Jr. has studied Eastern Psychology, Buddhist Healing, and Non-Violence at the Doctoral Level, credentials which should raise the eyebrow of interest in this newest of his books NOW. Singer has mastered the art of communication simply by confronting his readers with his warm but demanding command of 'Do it Now'. A Great Read… and one the reader will return to very frequently!"
Grady Harp
Amazon.com

"A storehouse of brief wisdom on the power of Now and staying open to the wonder of life, lovingly collected and interpreted. Read once a day!"
Tom Butler-Bowdon
Author of 50 Self-Help Classics, 50 Spiritual Classics

"Anyone who is seeking down-to-earth inspiration will find it in this compelling and accessible book."
Soulscode.com

"Richard manages to bring the Now to us in easy, practical, enjoyable bite size tasty 'moment-ary' morsels. I found myself melting into the quotes and stories on each page."
Tobias Lars
Spiritual Teacher and founder of SpiriTravel.com
& CourseOfAwakening.com

"Richard Singer's new book 'Now' reminds us that every breath we take is just as important as that first one we took at birth. Filled with personal stories from fascinating contributors, easy to follow reflections and exercises, 'Now' gives us the power back that we deserve, so we can embrace every moment and live a life that's vibrant, aware, happy and brimming with love."
Lisa D. Smith
'Quality of Life' Magazine & Radio

Contents

Foreword

When I wrote my first book, *Simple Truth*, way back in the last century, I was surprised that more than a couple of publishers told me that it was too short for them to consider publishing. Eventually, I published it myself and, after all these years, *Simple Truth* continues to sell as well as any of my [longer] books. More importantly, one of the most consistent responses from readers is that they appreciate its brevity.

I am a fan of concision; I love it when an author cuts to the chase and gives it to me straight. Don't try to impress me, just tell me, and show me what you've got.

Richard Singer is a man who not only understands the value of being concise, but is also extremely talented at transforming ideas and concepts, that others seem to make complex for complexity's sake, into beautifully written gems of wisdom. That's pretty cool all by itself, but Richard takes this a giant step beyond expressions of philosophical insight, and gives us utilitarian philosophy. What you hold in your hands is both a thought-provoking collection of reflections *and* a serious box of tools for anyone with the desire and intent to actually learn the practice of living in the moment.

But be warned: even the simplest tool requires repetitive practice if we expect mastery. There is nothing simpler than driving a nail with a hammer. But if you think that you are adept at driving nails, I encourage you to challenge a master carpenter to a nail driving competition.

So dive in — enjoy what Richard has to teach. And if you are ready to be a serious student of living in the moment, there is no time like the present to begin. Start *NOW*.

Thom Rutledge
Author of *Embracing Fear: How to Turn What Scares Us into Our Greatest Gift* (Harper Collins)

Author's Note and Introduction

When I reflect upon my writing, I realize what an incredible gift it is to share the knowledge that I have been given by so many great teachers throughout history. To express my thoughts of Truth, and realize my purpose, is the greatest opportunity I have ever had in life. There is no better feeling than to know that I have helped someone grow or achieve peace in their life. One such experience comes to mind. The experience will never escape me and I think this is one of the main reasons that I continue writing. The simple yet profound experience happened when I received a letter from a prisoner in Georgia who I had never met, seen or spoken to before. I opened the letter not knowing what to expect, or the reason it had been sent to me. All I know is that when I read it I felt an immense warmth flow through my body and at that point realized the reason that I wrote *Eastern Wisdom for Your Soul*. This one personal reason made the book worthwhile and I knew that my purpose was accomplished.

The letter was from an older gentleman who read my book while lying in his cell in a maximum-security prison. How my book ended up there I will never know, but what I do know is that it was right where it was supposed to be. This gentleman shared that my book had transformed his life and gave him the meaning that he needed to make it through his sentence. He consistently stated that the book gave him a way to free himself from despair and he promised himself he was going to live a life filled with peace. That is why I write. I believe my message needs to be shared with at least one person in the Universe. If my books reach that one person, I am satisfied because one person can share a message of peace and it will travel the entire world many times. Thank you for letting me share one more book with you, the most important person in the Universe.

The book you have in your hands is another gift that I was given and I want to share it with you. It contains a simple, yet profound message that has the power to change lives and transform humanity. *Now* is a book of 99 reflections along with several inspiring and practical essays with the single purpose of helping the reader make the most of the only moment they are given. Each reflection is written to be read separately, one day at a time while fully practicing the message contained within. This book is not meant to be read from cover to cover and then put on a shelf. That is useless and my purpose contained within is to be useful and transformative. You may find the reflections repetitive and that is alright. Repetition is the only way we learn and are able to break through our stubborn ego. Be patient, stay in the moment and allow the words to enter your life completely.

I wrote this book for you because I know the immense joy that living in the *Now* offers me in my life and I wanted to freely give this experience to you and all of humanity.

I specifically feel intense peace from the little things in life. This peace and tranquility comes to me when I am aware of the moment and become one with what is directly in front of me. I must admit that I enter the eternal present through simple yet extremely pleasurable tasks such as feeding my fish and watching them freely flow through the waters that surround them, or watering my Bonsai tree as I realize that I am connected to each leaf and blossoming flower. When I gaze at the stars at night I enter the eternal and these are the experiences that I want you to have. I hope you enjoy the gift I present you and experience the joy that lives only in the *Now*.

Go forth and attach your individual meaning and purpose to this book. I look forward to sharing the miracles that manifest in your life by living in the *Now*.

RAS
Grand Cayman, Cayman Islands

Dedication

This book is dedicated to my nephew who knew exactly how to live in the *Now*. He has departed us, but I know he encourages us all to live passionately in the present.

Edward R. Kenzakoski III
It is not the length of life, but the depth of life.
Ralph Waldo Emerson

If there was one soul in this world that lived deeply it was Ed Kenzakoski. Everything he was involved in was a passionate and spontaneous adventure. His life was a journey overflowing with dedication and persistence. Tasks that "average" people would give up on were challenges to Ed. He successfully completed and would persevere through anything and everything placed in his path. Courage came naturally and fear did not exist in his personal philosophy of living.

When Ed was born, a great adventure began. He touched the heart of everyone close to him and continued to do this throughout his lifetime. During his early childhood years he amazed everyone around him by hopping on a bike at nine months old, climbing towering trees at just a few years old, and becoming a great little wrestling champion when he was five. Ed always needed to be at the top and explore the Universe around him. He possessed an incredible mind, heart and soul. Ed knew no limits from the very beginning. He did not worry, he did not fear; he was simply a special and unique human being who innately knew that life needed to be lived spontaneously and adventurously in the present moment.

As Ed grew up he touched even more people around him and engaged in many more activities that he enjoyed deeply. He adored nature and spent as much time as possible communing with the outdoors. He was one with the natural world. The great outdoors was his limitless playground. Whether it was hunting, fishing, quadding, or just sitting in the woods; nature was his home.

Ed simply loved life. He loved and cared for everyone around him and would give his life for his loved ones. Passion for everyone and everything was Ed's existence. Work, fitness, family, friends, and the entirety of life, lived within Ed's heart and he expressed it in his own way in everything he did.

Now that Ed has departed this earth, you may think that something has changed. But, for those who knew and loved him, we are sure he is living even more of an adventure watching over us, making sure we are safe, and encouraging us to live life as passionately and courageously as he always did. Ed continues his journey and invites all of us to live our journey as deeply as possible. Ed lives on; feel him, love him, and listen to the message he lived in his passion-filled years.

Keep Ed's spirit alive by visiting his website at www. EdKenzWildandFree.com

My One and Only Son. My Heart and Soul, My World, My Everything.

I was lost walking this Earth until you found me, and now almost 24 years later, I am lost once again. You lived so fully in the *Now* and didn't allow the past or future to cloud your mind. You enjoyed your life fully, but one day your overwelming pain took its toll on your heart and you left this world and me, so quickly and tragically. The depression alone didn't cause the end; it was the alcohol that you chose to help cover that pain. All you could think of or feel was the pain at that moment. You felt helpless and had to escape the torture. If only you would have talked about it and accepted some help. If only...........
I'll have "if only's" running through my head for the rest of my life.

To all the readers:

Please! For me! And for every mother, father, grandparent, sibling, best friend, cousin, aunt, uncle, fiance, husband or wife, if you suffer from depression or any psychological disease don't try to mask your pain with alcohol or drugs. Please find it inside your being to talk to someone and find the help you need, so you can keep living in this precious moment. I have no more *Now* with my son, all I have is the past which I am truly grateful for because they are wonderful memories. They are wonderful all because we did live in the *Now* and enjoyed our time together... I'd give anything just for one more *Now*!

This book you have in your hands is very special to me and my whole family. I want to thank all of my friends and family who helped to make it possible. My son's memory will eternally live through it. Thank you all from the bottom of my heart!

Truly enjoy my Brother's newest book that your about to embark on. Pass it on and share it with the entire world. Most importantly, always remember that *Now* is truly all that we have!! In honor and memory of my son, Edward Raymond Kenzakoski III

His Mother Always, Sandy.

Part I

99 Present Centered Meditations

1.

Of all the days in our lives, which is the one that never comes?
Tomorrow. But we put everything off until then.
Paulo Coelho

Is this the case in your own life? Do you endlessly procrastinate and believe that one day you will begin living your dreams? If you are similar to the majority of human beings on this planet, this is precisely what you do. It is astonishing how many people plan to be happy tomorrow, when in fact that delusional day will never appear. No matter how long you wait, it will never be tomorrow. The only time to be happy, peaceful, successful or joyous is *Now*; this present moment is all that will ever be. If you desire to do something it must be initiated this very moment.

Do It Now

Begin to live this essential truth and make the most of each moment you are given starting *Right Now*. Your task today is to initiate something you have dreamed of doing all of your life. This may be writing a book, starting a charity, going back to school, volunteering at a nursing home or simply growing and expanding spiritually. You know what your heart desires, so begin the process and allow the Universe to walk beside you during this new journey. Throughout this book you will have an opportunity to put this into action. Use this precious time wisely and allow what lies within you to manifest in your life.

2.

Let us try to recognize the precious nature of each day.
His Holiness the Dalai Lama

Let us take this quote a bit further and realize the precious nature of each moment. This moment is all we are ever guaranteed. Life equals this moment and nothing more. Time is a dangerous illusion that deprives us of the pure bliss that fills the *Now*. Enlightened living takes place entirely in the *Now* and nowhere else. Rid yourself of the destructive past and the worrisome future, and dive into the infinite waters of the present.

Do It Now

Immerse yourself into what is in front of you with all your consciousness. Should anything else begin to flood your mind, quickly acknowledge it and let it go. *Right Now* is all you need to concern yourself with. Mindfulness of the task at hand can turn the ordinary experience into an extraordinary adventure. Whatever you do today, do it with your entire being. This is the only way you can guarantee that you are living authentically.

3.

People in the west are always getting ready to live.
Alan Watts

Western society embraces the idea that our goal is to prepare to live life at some future time. People's lives are filled with meaningless monotonous tasks in order to live "someday." What makes us think or believe that we will ever be ready to live if we cannot give ourselves to the present moment and simply live *Now*? Living continues to be something that we push away until our lives are over. We intend to make life meaningful in the future, but in reality never even begin to truly make life meaningful in the present.

Do It Now

What future are you preparing for if the only time that exists is *Now*? Beware of following a society that is slowly destroying itself. There exists plenty of evidence that the majority that we call "normal" has no clue how to live effectively or in peace. Make a conscious effort *Right Now* to stop pushing life away and embrace it with all the zest and energy that resides within the core of your being.

4.

To the dull mind all of nature is leaden. To the illuminated mind the whole world sparkles with light.
Ralph Waldo Emerson

The Universe gives us a choice concerning how we decide to experience the world. We can be enchanted and amazed by the phenomena that surrounds us and be mindful of the precious gifts that the Universe provides us with or, alternatively, we can walk the earth ignoring all the splendor of our surroundings. The true beauty and astonishment in life originates within your spirit. Whether you choose to connect your life to this source or merely walk alone with your ego is probably the most influential decision you will ever make

Do It Now

Open your eyes and your heart to the immense beauty that surrounds you. See things like it is the first time and allow your being to fuse with all things. The natural beauty of life is one with your soul. Be and feel the wind, the water, the sun and enter into its divinity. You are one with all. We are all creations of the Universal Intelligence.

5.

Precious and rare opportunities surround us, and we should recognize their value.
His Holiness the Dalai Lama

Our "normal" daily melodramatic lives overshadow the miraculous that surrounds us. To become one with the beauty contained in the Universe, it is imperative that you wade through the dense fog of delusion and welcome the truth of the Universe in all areas of your life. Miracles are an everyday occurrence when we live with mindfulness and according to our soul; but miracles cease to exist when we are caught in the entrapment of the ego.

Do It Now

Be mindful and alert to the signs in your daily life. Walk slowly and look around noticing all the wonders of the Universe. Allow your ego to disappear into the background and consciously experience everything along your path.

6.

We must have courage to face whatever is present.
Jack Kornfield

Fear is merely an illusion fabricated by our ego to stop us from truly manifesting our true purpose and meaning in life. All that is contained within us is within our reach when we decide to stop paying attention to the ego and travel forward with courage and faith in the Universe. The ego's foremost goal is to hold us back from peace and from living a fulfilled life. If you choose to follow the ego, you are abandoning the perfect life that is meant for you. If you choose otherwise you are in for an exciting adventure.

Do It Now

Only you can stop the unfolding of pure bliss in your life. It is you who allows the ego to sabotage your life. And it is you who can throw the ego's chains aside and run freely. Shed these chains *Now* and celebrate your new found independence.

7.

In spite of your fear do what you have to do.
Chin-Ning Chu

Fear prohibits us from following our divine path. We remain in our safe and comfortable world even though our internal wisdom is telling us to move on and embrace risks; to stand up and break out of our self-imposed cage of comfort and pursue the rewards that await us. There is only one simple decision that holds you back and that decision is to allow yourself to feel the fear and move through it with courage and determination; this decision needs to be made right this moment. No more procrastinating!

Do It Now

Make the life changing decision *Now* to face your illusive ego-created demons head on and pursue what belongs to you before it is too late. The feelings of fear only last as long as you allow them to inhabit your mind. Once you begin taking action without thinking about the fear it subsides and you become its conqueror.

8.

Our life is frittered away by detail....simplify, simplify.
Henry David Thoreau

Our overly analytical psyche often takes away the beauty of life by overcomplicating everything in its path. This may make us feel intellectual, in control, powerful and superior, but it also does one other important thing; it takes away the quintessence of life and our ability to be in harmony with our innate spiritual beings. Spirituality cannot be analyzed, defined, or produced in the intellect; spirituality is a simple feeling that we must allow ourselves to experience and sense rather than characterize within our mind. Stop thinking so obsessively today and allow your spirit to breathe.

Do It Now

Allow your overly analytical mind to take a break and simply enjoy the magnificence of this moment. This moment is filled with natural love and peace compared to the neuroticism of your mindless ego. If you don't enjoy the experience of simplicity and living in the moment, the fast paced, intellectual, over analyzing life awaits your return with a devilish smirk.

9.

If you can spend a perfectly useless afternoon in a perfectly useless manner, you have learned how to live.

Lyn Yutang

Structured living, endless to-do lists, rigid plans, expectations and deadlines all take away from the spontaneous and audacious nature of our being. Within us exists an energy that desperately desires to be unleashed and manifested in the outside world. This force can only experience freedom if we begin to live spontaneously and without the restraints created by society. Life is meant to be lived freely, *Right Now.*

Do It Now

Allow the gates of the ego to open and simply try planning an unplanned day for once and follow the path that your heart leads you on.

10.
I couldn't wait for success so I went ahead without it.
Jonathon Winters

Many individuals sit around and wait for their so-called time in the spotlight, their great break at last, and the fortune and fame that they feel they deserve in life. The fact in life is that if you continue using this strategy you may be waiting a dreadfully long time. Stand up and take responsibility for creating and discovering the success you deserve in life. It all comes from personal responsibility and taking action toward your goals and desires. If you wait around you may be giving up your opportunity for success. Find success and run with it with all the persistence and enthusiasm the Universe has provided you.

Do It Now

Leave the baggage of your ego behind as you sprint full force for the success you deserve. The doubts, criticisms, and negativity of your ego and the people around you do not really exist, so drop them and go freely onward toward the rewards that await you.

11.
Live as if you were to die tomorrow.
Gandhi

Life purely consists of the present moment. *Right Now* is truly all you possess and all you will ever possess within your life. If you desire to genuinely live, you must immerse yourself as deeply as you can within this moment. Experiencing an awakening and achieving illumination are only accomplished by allowing your being to be filled with the elucidation and bliss of the *Now*. Everything other than the *Now* is merely a misapprehension that distorts your capacity to truly live serenely in the present.

Do It Now

Do you desire to die without ever genuinely feeling as though you were finally beginning to live? Let go of the attachments of the past and the desires of the future and simply *Be, Right Here, Right Now.*

12.
Suffering is resistance to what is.
Stephen Levine

Absolute acceptance of what is and what isn't in our life at this instant is our key to peace, tranquility, and independence from all suffering. Each and every situation and challenge that we encounter in life is precisely the way it is supposed to be. If you follow your Universal path and heed all the lessons presented to you in each moment, you will release yourself from the bondage of what you think your life should be, and allow yourself to be completely at peace with what actually is. This is authentic living.

Do It Now

Ask the Universe for the courage to accept life as it is and make the most of each individual learning experience that you encounter. Every moment has something unique that you can use in your own personal growth process.

13.

For true success ask yourself these four questions: Why?; Why not?; Why not me?; Why not now?
James Allen

Success is rather straightforward if you rid yourself of all the negative energy that has been built up inside you for years. Stop doubting and start believing, stop criticizing and start commending, stop worrying and start acting, and stop procrastinating and start achieving. All of this is within your reach if you only believe in your purpose and your worthiness as a unique, exceptional and talented human being. Move forward *Now* and achieve the inherent greatness that lives within you.

Do It Now

Start believing in yourself and begin fulfilling all your desires. Recognize that all the people who fulfilled their purpose and dreams are made up of the exact substance that makes you. There is no difference between you and every human being that achieved prominence throughout history, except they believed, acted, and followed through with perseverance and dedication.

14.

It is better to live one day ethically and reflectively than to live a hundred years immoral and unrestrained.
Buddha

One ethical and well-lived day giving your inner gifts to humanity can change the world; one day engaged in a careless and depraved lifestyle can destroy the world. It is not the length or duration of your life you should concern yourself with, it is how many days or moments you bestow to other human beings that measures your level of success. We are definitely not here to count the years; the main principle of our existence is to count the acts of pure kindness that we offer humanity.

Do It Now

Focus all your energy on how you can make a difference in the world. Prepare a written plan that you can implement within the next year. Include what changes you will attempt to make and how you will contribute your little piece to transforming the world. Do this and you will witness the joy that you can experience by stepping out of your comfortable little box and giving to humanity. Don't wait, because the right time will never come.

15.

My philosophy is that not only are you responsible for your life, but doing the best at this moment puts you in the best place for the next moment.
Oprah Winfrey

Life is made up of a compilation of solitary present moments that provide you with the opportunity to start over and experience a rebirth each day. If we strive for excellence in every moment we are bound to create success in our life. Factually speaking, you have control and responsibility for how you, and only you, act in each moment of each day. This is all you control in life. It is up to you to decide what you do *Now*. If you decide to choose excellence and nothing less in each moment you will manifest brilliance and nothing less in the future of your life.

Do It Now

Evaluate your life up until this point: Do you take responsibility for where you are and who you have become, or do you blame others? Do you do your best in every moment you are given? Beginning *Now*, ensure that you take accountability for you and begin giving your best to each moment. If you choose to blame others and live a lazy existence, then the results will speak for themselves.

16.
**You will never change your life until you change something
you do daily. The secret of your success is found in your daily
routine.**
John C. Maxwell

Life is merely made up of distinct precious moments just like this
one right *Now*. These moments added together develop into days.
This concept is very straightforward, yet profound. The secret of
success is to do something each moment and each day that will
change your life. Develop a positive daily routine to get you where
you want to go. You will be pleasantly surprised with the results
this simple modification will produce.

Do It Now

Decide what aspects of your life you will choose to change and
embark on these changes *Now*. It is most effective to do this in
writing and keep it where you will see it on a consistent basis.

17.

Nature does not hurry, yet everything is accomplished.
Lao Tzu

Be patient at present and allow the Universe to guide you. Rid yourself of the urgency and the anxiety that pervades your days and allow yourself to feel the innate stillness of the Universe. Life was not created to be full of exigency, angst, hatred, fear, worry, or any of the other detrimental energies that bombard us on a daily basis. Humans created this way of life; society continues to live this way and we just tag along like helpless chicks following their mother. Come back to the natural course of the Universe and rejoice in the peace and tranquility of life. You do not need to take part in society's chaotic philosophy of living.

Do It Now

Right Now allow the innate flow of the Universe to guide you and witness the peace this way of life brings. Live along with nature, and all the negativity that is present in your life will pass without restricting your precious flow of energy. Follow this path and you will come alive.

18.

There is only one problem with saving your dream for someday.
Someday will always remain in the future.
Anonymous

Whatever your dreams may be, start to realize them *Now*. Give yourself what you deserve today. If you dream to go to a tropical island, plan the trip. If you want to change careers, start the process. This life is yours and it is intended to be a magnificent voyage. Open your mind and get rid of the fortifications that prevent you from experiencing your imaginings and soul-felt desires. Begin to take action to live the life you are destined to live. Visualize the results and goals, sense success deep within you, and truly recognize that you can have anything you yearn for as long as you have the passion and determination to discover your tremendous abilities and power in life.

Do It Now

Go forth *Now* and manifest all the dreams that your being desires. Begin to visualize your dreams and use all your senses to feel and experience meeting your highest goals. Your dreams will come true if you stop sabotaging yourself and let life guide you along the journey.

19.

Few people have the imagination for reality.
Goethe

Those individuals that have ever given themselves completely to the reality of simply *being*, understand this quote completely. However, you must know that you can never comprehend this with the mind. It is only comprehensible through direct experience in the moment. It is beyond logic, beyond teaching, and way beyond the ego. Reality is nothing like the description or perception we feed ourselves. Reality is perfection, beauty, abundance, and pure peace. However, don't listen to me, go forth and experience the miraculous yourself.

Do It Now

Right Now, your ego is most likely thinking that this is complete nonsense. Your ego exclaims, "Nothing exists that I do not know!" You can very easily conclude your search with your acceptance of the ego's words, and that is alright. Or you can move forward and journey into the unknown to experience life's true reality. I suggest not limiting yourself, especially based on the ego. I'm quite certain you are aware of the ego's track record in your own life.

20.

It is a mistake to look too far ahead. Only one link in the chain of destiny can be handled at a time.

Winston Churchill

There exist human beings who have not dealt with the past and continue to feel regret and guilt, and obsess about the impossible task of altering the past the way they desire it to be *Now*. There are also human beings who worry endlessly about the future and its uncertainty. If you continue to live, or rather exist, this way it is certain that you will not align with your higher purpose because this purpose lives in the present moment. Everything authentic and of value lives in the present. Begin to work on the present link in your destiny and discard the regrets of the past and the worries of the future; your life is *Now*.

Do It Now

Think honestly about the amount of time each day you spend in the past and the future. This time spent is entirely futile and unproductive. You are missing life! At this moment commit yourself to being mindful of how you use your time and whenever your ego takes you for an extensive murky walk in the past or a worthless flight into the future dismiss this nonsense and bring yourself back to where life really is. Past and future do not really exist; discontinue this insane behavior and live *Now*.

21.

Do not take lightly small good deeds, believing they can hardly help. For drops of water, one by one, in time can fill a giant pot.
Patrul Rinpoche

One of the truths in life that I continuously experience is that effective and successful living is achieved by breaking everything down into minute pieces. Whether it's writing a book, achieving a major life goal, or saving humanity it can only be done one step at a time. We do not possess a magic wand that we wave and great feats are instantly accomplished. If we look at anything closely throughout history that was achieved by human beings, we will be presented with an extensive struggle of small, but persistent, steps that eventually leads to success if we are determined and never give up.

Do It Now

Begin doing small things in your life and you will eventually reach your desired goal. However, you must keep in mind that there is no success in life unless it has a connection to helping your fellow human beings. Break everything down into manageable steps in your mind and in physical practice and great success awaits you.

22.

The greatest revelation is stillness.
Lao Tzu

Be still and experience the natural ecstasy of this sacred moment. Embrace the all-pervading Universal Energy that surrounds you and allow it to penetrate your entire being. This bliss you feel is the genuine nature of life. Remember that this dynamic force is constantly available to you; you must simply allow it to enter and fuse within the heart of your authentic being.

Do It Now

Sit in nature for an extended period of time and concentrate entirely on the connection of your breath and the atmosphere that surrounds you. This is the energy of the Universe. You are this source. If you are tranquil and unite with the invisible energy of the cosmos, you will see, feel and become one with this miraculous force.

23.

It's time to start living the life you imagined.
Henry James

Human beings often take advantage of, and ignore, the precious nature of life and the potential it contains. If you are just merely getting by or existing in a tedious life, please reflect and contemplate the exceptional opportunity you have and the inexhaustible possibilities that are right in front of you. Whatever you can envision or dream, you can create in your life. Believe and take action and you will experience astounding results. Wash away the debris of the ego and the deception of society and tap into the truth and innocence that you once enjoyed. Go and challenge life for what you believe.

Do It Now

Return to the innocence of youth and live the adventures that once filled your unadulterated mind. Challenge the mediocrity and monotonous in life, and have fun in this world that passes away much too quickly. You are a child of the Universe; join the adventure and achieve incredible things.

24.

The question is not whether we will die, but how we will live.
Joan Borysenko

Death is inevitable; however, life is a choice that we make on a daily basis. We can choose to live today or merely exist and waste precious time. You will eventually die and move on, but will you merely exist in life or will you live genuinely and courageously? This is truly up to you and only you. Tap into your internal resources and craft the life of your dreams. It is your time to shine in the enlightenment of the Universe.

Do It Now

Our only choice right this moment is how we choose to spend it. We never know if we will get another moment similar to this one, so what are you going to do with this unique moment? It is entirely up to you.

25.

**What we think of as 'sacred' actually is present in
everything we do.**
Riane Eisler

If you look at life in a thorough and sincere manner, you will recognize how sacred everyone and everything is around you. Everything we see, do, and come into contact with is sacred; however, society has attempted to obliterate the sacred within the Universe. Take back your ability to recognize and feel everything as unique and special and dance in the elegance of life. Each moment of each day is precious and needs to be appreciated for its pure essence.

Do It Now

Take back the purity of life and embrace the creation and innovativeness of all the simple things that surround you. Step out of the repetitive, robotic habits of society and see things as they truly are. Go outside and gaze at the infinity of the heavens above and you will once again return to the innocent state that has the power to awaken you.

26.

The ideal day never comes. Today is ideal for him who makes it so.

Horatio Dresser

We often hear many people express that "someday they will be happy." They are going to be happy when they find a new job, get an advanced university degree, find a perfect lover. Why not take advantage of this very moment and make this the day you decide to be peaceful, happy, and filled with gratitude for what does exist in your life? Future happiness is a goal that will not be achieved if present happiness is not a priority. Absolutely nothing external has the power to make you happy; happiness must be a choice decided from within.

Do It Now

Do yourself a favor and make "someday" manifest today in your life. It will never be the future, thus you cannot postpone your happiness and peace until then. Yes, society and capitalism tells you that you need more and more and more to be successful and content, however look around and see how erroneous society truly is. External riches or achievements will never allow you to possess what you really desire. You become fulfilled and at peace from within

27.

When mindfulness shines its light upon our activity, we recover ourselves and encounter life in the present moment. The present moment is a wonderful moment.

Thich Nhat Hanh

Mindfulness can be compared to the radiance and life-giving qualities of the sun. Without sunlight we die, and without mindfulness we exist as if we were deceased. We only truly begin to live when we allow the illumination of the present moment to penetrate our lives. Everything else is in conflict with truly being alive. Indeed the present moment is a wonderful moment, but it is really the only moment. If you are not in the *Now* you are not in the Light. And if you are not in the Light you exist in the darkness.

Do It Now

Can you accurately see anything in the dark? No, we must shine a light on our path in order to journey forward. Well stop trying to navigate in the darkness and allow light to enter your life. If you wish, you may flip the switch at anytime and mindfulness will be there to shine its lamp upon your path.

28.

Each today well lived, makes yesterday a dream of happiness, and each tomorrow a vision of hope. Look, therefore to this one day, for it and it alone is life.

Sanskrit Poem

Not many of us choose to genuinely live life. We often choose to live what others tell us life is or how others dictate us to live. They foolishly tell us to live for the future, regret the past, and worry about what may or may not come. They may not all express this directly; however, they do show us subtly by their actions and behavior. When you look around, how many individuals do you see embracing the experience of the moment, enjoying what's in front of them, or simply being happy to be alive? I know, personally, I do not see many.

Do It Now

Be the one in the crowd that is "being" rather than rushing. Enjoy what is and begin to practice this "secret ritual" in your everyday living. Abandon the majority and allow yourself to experience the gift of awareness.

29.

The unhappiest of mortals is that man who insists upon reliving the past, over and over in imagination—continually criticizing himself for past mistakes—continually condemning himself for past sins."
Maxwell Maltz

Freedom from the past is only accomplished by your own doing. You and you alone have the choice and ability to either torture yourself for being human or forgive yourself for your mortality and imperfection. This is when you will truly be able to live in the present moment where life really exists. Forgiveness of yourself is necessary if you plan to have peace, serenity, and any form of genuine happiness. Allow yourself to heal the pain of the past and move along your course to tranquility and joyous living. It is quite senseless to continue to permit the past, which cannot be changed, to dictate your present state of living. If you feel the need to experience guilt, remorse, and regret, that's fine; however, experience it once or twice, learn the lesson intended and move forward. There is no productivity in feeling this pain 147,000 times over a 30-year period.

Do It Now

Forgive yourself *Right Now* by writing down the details of how the past is chaining you there and taking life away from you each and every moment. Discuss this list with someone you trust and then burn it as a sacred ritual and your rebirth will begin *Right Now* in this very moment. The more you project the past upon the present, the more miserable and caged you will become. The fact remains that you did the best you could with what you had at any given time in the past.

30.

Nothing is left to you at this moment but to have a good laugh.

Zen Saying

Our entire organism heals with laughter. We connect to humanity and develop relationships through humor and laughing together. We lose track of time and become immersed in the moment when our being is blissful with laughter. Laughter is a mind-body medicine that can teach you what life is all about. Laugh and you will experience the *Now* in completeness.

Do It Now

Attention: Being too serious is hazardous to your health! Be sure to give yourself a dose of laughter each day. Actually give yourself several doses of laughter and you will feel its miraculous curative effect. Laughter is therapy and medicine all wrapped in one. Laugh at yourself and life often. Being too serious can cause toxic stress, being too humorous can cause joyous living. You decide.

31.
You can't build a reputation on what you're going to do.
Henry Ford

Never listen to the doubts and criticism of your ego. Move forward and take the necessary steps to accomplish your goals. Action is the key to success. Many individuals discuss and plan success their whole lives, but they never act upon their intentions and they are left with nothing but regret when they realize that they have procrastinated much too long. Take small but consistent steps and you will accomplish what you set out to do.

Do It Now

In staying with what you identified in previous meditations, continue to take the steps in achieving your goals and if you haven't started yet, what are you waiting for? Answer this question *Right Now*: If you believed you could accomplish anything, what would it be? Start it *Now* and visualize the internal knowledge that you can achieve anything you wish. Your ability and competence is not holding you back, it is merely the false thoughts of your ego that puts your dreams on hold.

32.

Do not dwell in the past; do not dream of the future, concentrate the mind on the present moment.

Buddha

We exert an abundant amount of powerful energy by attempting to live in the illusions of the past and the projections of the future. The past and the future do not exist, thus we must conserve our energy for the all-important *Now*. Do not waste precious moments on regrets, worries, obsessions or any other thoughts that deprive you of immersion in the present moment. Release your unproductive thoughts and allow your spirit to graciously soar in the eternal present.

Do It Now

Free yourself from the chains of your past and future thoughts and allow the divine breeze to carry you through the day. Spread your wings and soar in the eternity that you now possess. Feel the divine embrace your body and soul; this is freedom.

33.

Freedom is nowhere to go, nothing to have, and nothing to be.
Stephen Levine

Enlightenment is achieved in a split second, at the moment when you are able to experience life completely in the *Now*, free from the past, future, sensory desires, and delusions. It is simply being free in the immensity of the *Here and Now*, and embracing your connection to all of humanity. Be one with the Universe without judgments, fear, worry, expectations or attachments. Transcend the separation of your ego and experience the feeling of what it is to *Be*, a feeling that you share with all things that surround you. Accept everything about this moment. It really is that simple, but we love to complicate it to no end.

Do It Now

Begin to apply this to your life slowly, but consistently. Give yourself permission to let go of the apprehensive voice of your ego and allow freedom to saturate your being. Plan nothing, buy nothing, covet nothing, and be no one other than your pure self. Spontaneously float through your day with no rigid plan or direction; just *Be* like the air that fills the Universe. Follow the soft whisper of your soul and bask in the liberation that it brings you. Remember - practice a little at a time, as this is quite a change from the artificial reality you have become accustomed to.

34.

For long years a bird in a cage, today, flying along with the clouds.

Zen Saying

Attachment surrounds us like the walls of a penitentiary. You may believe you are free, but your ego makes sure you are enslaved by its demands. Everything in life we are attached to joins in to imprison us to the external rather than being free within and without. To release this heavy burden, and escape the shackles, we must connect with all things. We must simply *Be* and allow our being to connect intimately with the water that flows, the air that we breathe, and all that is natural and genuine.

Do It Now

The delusions and cravings that keep you in bondage must be brought into the light of reality. Once we shine the light of truth on these meaningless desires, they can no longer keep us trapped. Take an inventory of what your ego is striving towards and honestly assess if these external and material things and achievements will set you free or keep you chained.

35.
It's right to be content with what you have, but not with
what you are.
Unknown Author

To be content and satisfied with who you are prevents growth in all areas of your life. It is reasonable and desirable to be at peace with yourself in each waking moment of life, however, you must always persist along your path incessantly and courageously looking within and searching for areas within yourself to cultivate. Self-growth will transform your way of living and create a life you can only imagine. Grow within and discover the personal power and the unlimited potential that inhabits your inner world.

Do It Now

Develop a comprehensive list of what you would like to change about yourself. If you search within there are many things within your being that can be improved. Work on each change individually in a patient but spirited manner. Nothing changes outside of you until your work is done internally. Remember this is a life long process and perfection is not possible, however steady growth is indeed a necessity.

36.

Cultivating an active mindfulness of ones experience, moment by moment, is the path to awakening.
Joseph Goldstein

Blissful living only takes place in this very moment. If you truly savor the moment, you will genuinely experience the reality and rapture that life has to offer. Life exists nowhere else but this moment; the past and the future are merely illusions of our psyche. Immerse yourself in this moment *Right Now* and awaken the ecstasy that patiently waits within you. Wake up and begin living today.

Do It Now

Mindfulness or present centered meditation is very straightforward. Begin to practice this by keeping your awareness in this very moment and allowing all other thoughts to drift away like the passing clouds. If you persist in this practice, your mind will eventually relax and the harmony will encircle your entire being.

37.

Past and future veil God from our sight; Burn up both of them with fire.

Rumi

Rumi speaks with intensity and immediacy when advising us through his words. This demonstrates the destructive force of both the past and the future in our present lives. Presence is the only place we will discover the divine source of the Universe. Forever dwell in the *Now* and you will be blessed eternally with ecstasy and joy. Live in the past and the future and you drown yourself in the dark sea of meaningless existence.

Do It Now

Make it a point today to set fire to the past and future in your life and allow the ashes to disappear with no expected return. This is the only way that you can take advantage of all that life holds for you. Stop wasting precious time focusing on what does not exist.

38.
Where do you live?
Young people live in the future.
Old people live in the past.
Wise people live in the present.
Unknown Author

Do you constantly dwell on the mistakes of the past, the regrets, and the emotional turmoil, or do you drown yourself in the uncertainties and the dread of the future? The only place that life can truly be enjoyed is in the *Now*. If you are in the past or the future, you are throwing away your experience of life and merely existing. The choice of where you live is of course yours; however, if you desire peace, serenity and contentment, the only place that has this accessible to you is *Right Now* in this exceptional moment.

Do It Now

The illumination and enlightenment of this very moment is readily available to you if you make the choice to accept it entirely. As always, the choice remains yours and can only be decided by taking the route of the wise, and undoing the egos' chains and stubborn opposition to life.

39.

The only way to deal with the future is to function efficiently in the now.

Gita Bellin

As a separate reality, the future does not exist. Although you can truly do nothing about your future you should realize that the current moments of your life add up to what the future becomes. The process of achieving excellence in the *Now* sets the momentum in your life to arrive at future excellence. *Right Now*, right here in this moment is the only way to create what you desire for yourself in the future. Live *Now*, achieve *Now*, and experience the present moment to the fullest. Immersion in the ocean of the present will allow your life to be in alignment with the harmony of the Universe.

Do It Now

Realistically there is no future in life. As I have pointed out many times the *Now* is all we ever have. However, if you wish to think of a future, the most accurate way to achieve what you wish is to do your very best in this moment. After all, what you think of as the future is simply a compilation of present moments.

40.

There is more to life than increasing its speed.

Gandhi

Life tends to speed up each and everyday that passes. The goal of society appears to be getting things done as expeditiously as possible and then to move on to the next monotonous meaningless task. We run around doing, doing, doing. Life is more than merely getting things done as fast as possible and eliminating your inexhaustible To-Do list. Embrace and honor the precious nature of life today and eliminate society's need for speed.

Do It Now

Make it a part of your To-Do list today to stop, slow down, cherish the wonders around you and allow yourself to recognize the preciousness of life's blissful journey. Look around and see the precision of a blade of grass, the miraculous quality of a cloud floating in the infinite sky, and the unbounded exquisiteness of nature.

41.
Whatever you can do, or dream you can, begin it.
Boldness has genius, power and magic in it.
Begin it now.
Goethe

There is no difference between you and all the other exceptional individuals throughout history who have achieved their greatest dreams and created the lives they imagined. You have this innate genius within you that is waiting to be born and waiting to give birth to a transformation in your life and the world. You have miracles housed within your being, and it is *Now* time to unleash them into the Universe.

Do It Now

If you can dream it, you can achieve it. There are so many people in this Universe who keep their dreams buried within their beings. This is not fair to humanity or the world. The Universe deserves to see and feel the product of your imagination. It is your duty to manifest that which will benefit the world. Wake up your unique genius and share it with all of humanity.

42.
Confine yourself to the present.
Marcus Aurelius

This is the secret we have been longing for since the beginning of time. This one principle, if followed and applied, will give you the peace you desire in your life. Begin living completely in the present moment. Remember, you are always in the *Now*; this is all you have control of. All the gifts and signs that the Universe has for you are presented right in this moment. Connection to life and the precious offerings are only available in the present. Listen, learn, enjoy, and find peace in this very moment. This is the secret that most human beings never benefit from due to their ego's need to attempt to change the past and control the future.

Do It Now

Will you allow this secret to pass you by? Are you willing to waste your life without applying this simple technique to living? Give the present a chance and see what it can offer you. I promise you will not be let down.

43.
Flow with whatever is happening and let your mind be free.
Stay centered by accepting whatever you are doing.
This is the ultimate.
Chuang Tzu

Mindfulness in the present moment is the key to absolute tranquility in life. Savor the radiance and splendor of this single moment in front of you. This is where you will discover your life's meaning. Live *Now* and become intimate with the present. Whatever it is that you attempt to do in your life today, remember to focus on the feelings it produces. Be conscious of each detail of your task and relish whatever it is you are experiencing. Excellence is sure to transpire if you put all of your energy, passion, and vitality into each specific task in each moment of your life.

Do It Now

Begin breaking the manacles of the ego and accept where you are and what you are doing *Right Now*; simply surrender to the precision of the moment and trust that you are exactly where you are supposed to be. This is perfection!

44.

To see the preciousness of all things, we must bring our full attention to life.
Jack Kornfield

We allow so many phenomenal moments to pass us by due to our distraction. All the essential and beautiful things seem to fall prey to the droning activities that we call life. Instead of entering the tunnel vision of our typical everyday routine, we need to go around that tunnel and open our eyes to the magnificence that is presented all around us. When is the last time you noticed the exquisiteness of the sky, or the bright welcoming smile of a stranger, or simply stopped in your tracks to open a door for someone or lend a helping hand to someone struggling? These are the things we need to pay attention to, not the money in our account, the car we drive, or the rising above another human being.

Do It Now

Stop and make it a point to do things different today. Just for today, make a special effort to interrupt your routine and open your eyes to the miracles of the Universe. Look at little things, spend more time in nature, do some good deeds when presented with the opportunity, and smile throughout the day. Keep your mind on that which doesn't even enter your attention in your standard routine. This simple practice will allow you to discover the Universe you left behind a long, long time ago.

45.
Rest your frontal lobe.
Dainin Katagiri

Why would you actually want to rest the part of your brain that analyzes everything? You tell me. Do you wish to live constantly thinking, analyzing, and scheduling everything you do without just simply enjoying life as it is. It certainly gets tiring trying to administer and direct the Universe. The frontal lobe has evolved over time so we can take control of our lives, but is this even possible or is it another human created illusory system that actually doesn't benefit us very much?

Do It Now

To control or not control? That is the question you must answer. Has your control and excessive planning worked out for you in your life or does it take away your ability to actually live and take pleasure in life in a spontaneous and natural manner? You must decide based on your experience which path you choose to follow.

46.

If a thing is worth doing, its worth doing well.
Chinese Proverb

Everything you do in your life deserves your undivided attention and 100% of your effort. This is the most effective way to seize the opportunities and miracles that avail themselves to you along your daily journey. Strive to engrave your unique and precious trademark on everything you pursue in life. This encompasses everything from washing the dishes to painting a masterpiece. Each moment of each task in life is sacred and should be treated this way. Simply to be healthy enough to wake up, take a shower, vacuum, and to complete all of the other so-called "ordinary" tasks in your life, is a miracle, and each of these tasks overflows with divinity.

Do It Now

Dedicate one entire day to focus all of your attention and energy on each and every task that you become involved in. Absorb yourself in each moment and each breath, and experience the ecstasy and power of the timeless present. Notice the energy that surrounds you, along with the serenity and tranquility of the Universe. Simply *Be*, and become one with whatever you are involved in. This is life. Your presence in the *Now* is as sacred as living gets.

47.

We can make a difference in our tomorrows provided we deliver nothing but the very best we can do, everyday.
Og Mandino

Worries about the future often prevent us from performing at our optimal level in the present moment. The simple, but profound, secret is that there is no need to worry about the future if you strive for excellence today, because what you do each day adds up to what your future becomes. Get on the path to excellence today and secure what the future holds for you. Be the finest human being you can be today and a phenomenal future will be patiently awaiting your arrival.

Do It Now

Strategically place a simple note or reminder on your desk so you can remember to be your very best each moment of the day. Develop a habit of focusing all your energy on the task in front of you and you will release the brilliance contained within your being.

48.
Opportunities are multiplied as they are seized.
Sun Tzu

Each moment of each day has embedded in it limitless opportunities for growth and development. Immerse yourself in the vast ocean of the *Now* and avail yourself to the infinite possibilities out there waiting for you. Each time you are successful in a task you take on, you will be presented with a subsequent gift from the Universe. You must keep your eyes open and follow the signs that are positioned upon your path.

Do It Now

"Coincidences" are plentiful in our lives, but are these occurrences merely coincidences? Unfortunately, your ego desires that you believe in the coincidence theory and quickly discard the events as chance happenings. Following your ego is the easiest way to be blind to the essential signs of the Universe. Behind these so-called "coincidental events", is the powerful and profound intelligence of creation. These are divine events created with the purpose of aligning you with the Ultimate Truth. You must keep the eyes of your soul open in order to bathe in the cosmic synchronicity. Connect to this source, and you will eternally walk the sacred path that is directly in front of your eyes.

49.
You already have the precious mixture that will make you well.
Use it.
Rumi

Obviously, our human need to seek external cures is not a phenomenon of modern times, if Rumi was speaking about it. We have always had the endless need to search outside for what abundantly exists within us. We search outside for happiness, pleasure, health, success, and peace. Do we search inside for anything? It's just like us humans to look past what has actually been within us always. Perhaps we are scared to look where we have never looked before. Trust me there is nothing to fear and only peace to discover. It's the outside world that's dangerous and the inside world is where we find our protection.

Do It Now

Take some time to delve within the depths of your being. This is the only place you have not searched. I'm quite sure you comprehensively searched your outer surroundings for all that you desire. Have you unearthed anything worthwhile yet? When will you put an end to this ineffective pursuit? I do hope it will be soon.

50.
If you were going to die soon and had only one phone call you could make, who would you call and what would you say? And why are you waiting?
Stephen Levine

Right this moment, who do you need to express your unconditional affection to? Who do you need to forgive, to apologize to, or just let them know you care? Contemplate for a moment that you might die at the end of the day today. Who will you contact today and what will you say? What business have you left unfinished in your life? Remember, you are only guaranteed this moment happening *Right Now*; your illusion of immortality is merely a dream; your last breath in this body may be just around the corner.

Do It Now

Call or visit the important people in your life. Make it a point to express your love for them as often as possible and stop taking these individuals for granted. Never wait until the future to allow the love and compassion of your heart to be manifested in the Universe. Live *Now* and you will eternally be grateful and free of regret. Today express appreciation to everyone you love.

51.

Life is what happens to you while you're busy making other plans.
John Lennon

We all know those people, or you may be one of them, who will surely experience happiness and contentment when they purchase a new home, a new car, get a high paying job, or go on their dream vacation. Unfortunately, when those things are accomplished happiness becomes nonexistent. Be happy and peaceful *Now* in this moment and stop forecasting happiness. Happiness is always created within, and then projected to the outside world. If you cannot be happy within, I am sorry to inform you that experiencing authentic contentment externally is not feasible.

Do It Now

Make a commitment to be happy *Right Now* in this very moment. It is you who chooses happiness not inanimate, future-based objects or accomplishments. Those things you base your happiness on in the future come and go and unfortunately, you will find additional material things to pursue. This is an ongoing, dreadful cycle that never ends until you decide personally to put an end to it once and for all.

52.
When you realize how perfect everything is you will tilt your head and laugh at the sky.
Buddha

It is not very difficult to recognize the exactitude contained within this miraculous Universe. You simply need to open the eyes of your soul, and gaze at the natural magnificence and impeccability of your surroundings. Perfection and harmony are available abundantly at this present moment; finding perfection is purely a matter of detaching from your egos' desires and bathing in the bliss-filled ocean of your natural existence.

Do It Now

Take an hour (or more) out of your day and look intently at every spectacular creation surrounding you in your natural environment. Look up at the sky and feel the awe-inspiring perfection it contains. Feel the soothing warmth of the sun or the brisk sensation of the fresh air. Look at the trees and follow their development back to a single seed; a single seed which has grown into splendid beauty. Tune into the vibration of the atmosphere and bathe in the phenomenal energy from which this Universe is made. Complete this exercise without the ego, without the rational mind, and without the conditioning you have been granted by society. Simply experience the *Nowness* of this very moment. Be one with all around you and lose yourself in the immensity of existence. This is perfection. No desires, no attachments, no expectations. Nowhere to go, nothing to be, absolutely nothing to do. Just experience what it is to exist in the perfection of the *Now*.

53.

The Ultimate state is ever present and always now.
Advashanti

Being unable to realize the ultimate power and importance of the *Now* is the greatest defect of the human ego. It is this deficiency that keeps us stuck in the obscurity of illusion. Our ego consistently and callously leads us astray as it follows the path of the delusion of time; this path chains us to the past and the future, which are never a reality. The journey of the ego offers nothing but endless regret, despair, anxiety, and an everlasting craving for external and impermanent desire. The journey of the eternal present, offers nothing but pure bliss, ecstatic experience and enlightenment. Like Ram Dass says, "Be here now."

Do It Now

Whether you like it or not, it is always *Now* and you are always here. Whether you choose to admit this and live in the moment, is, and has always been, up to you. You can remain in the delusion of time and suffer or you can be present in the *Here and Now,* knowing peace. The 'secret' to life is not a secret. It has been suggested by many people in many ways since the beginning of time: "Live in the *Now*"; "Be present"; "The present is a gift"; "Today is all you have"; and so forth. The issue simply is that we hear these words and say, "Wow, that's true", and then we allow this truth to escape us, returning to the mirage of the world. Well, here it is again, the secret that is not a secret; immerse yourself in the present moment and you will be free. Apply it to your life if you desire to be liberated, or choose not to and return to your cell of delusion and remain trapped.

54.

Every moment of your life is infinitely creative and the Universe is endlessly bountiful. Just put forth a clear enough request, and everything your heart desires must come to you.

Gandhi

You probably do not realize how enormously potent you actually are. Within your being lies the infinite power of the Universe. You have the potential to manifest your deepest dreams and heart felt desires. This enormous capacity lies dormant within your being until you make a sincere decision to tap into it. This does not make you superior. It simply unites you with the energy of creation which all human beings possess but, unfortunately, rarely utilize in their lives. The Universe is you and you are the Universe. Directly align and communicate with this power, and you will become one with the love and harmony that lies at the foundation of all creation. Become the human being that you are meant to be, and allow the peace and bliss of the Universe to saturate every particle of your being. Be the *You* that has always been a part of your heart. This is in your power, so make the decision and enjoy the extraordinary journey.

Do It Now

Tap into the immense power of your being and begin imagining and visualizing all that your heart desires. The Universe will work in unison with you and will guarantee you achieve what your entire being desires. You must first ask the creative energy to help you, take the appropriate action, and follow through with persistence and dedication. You can have what you want as long as it will help humanity in its transformation process.

55.

No matter how hard the past, one can always begin again today.
Buddha

Today is all we ever have. In fact, this moment *Right Now* is all that you ever really possess in your entire life. Life equals *Now*. It's that simple. If you sit and sincerely contemplate this, you will realize that you are never truly guaranteed the next moment. Your mind is determined to consistently place your attention deep within the past or far into the future. Both of these (living in the moments of the past or dreaming of the moments of the future) are illusions that destroy the reality of the present. Detach yourself from the faulty guidance of your mind and simply allow yourself to *Be* in the radiance of the *Now*. This is where living takes place; it does not exist anywhere but in the present.

Do It Now

When your thoughts wander aimlessly away from the present, attaching themselves to the pain and regret of the past, simply remind yourself that all you have and all that matters is the *Eternal Now*. The more you practice this the more you will become alive and filled with the light of the presence rather than being weighed down with the darkness of the past and future.

56.

Meditate and realize this world is filled with the presence of God.

Upanishads

Look around and immerse yourself in the cascade of silence and tranquility of the Universe. Basking in the light of the present will help you realize the Truth. Focus on and become one with the mysterious beauty of the sky, the innocence and love of your family, the compassion of your friends and the power and illumination of the products of creation.

Do It Now

God is within us and is that omnipotent and all loving source that connects everything. Write down and contemplate the unique and immensely powerful characteristics of your personal God and begin to connect to this perfect energy.

57.
If you want to be a writer, stop talking about it and sit down and write.
Jackie Collins

Many people spend their life sitting around talking about what they want to be, what they want to do, and how life would be much better if they were doing this and that. If you are this type of person you must sit, think, and deeply contemplate what you want to accomplish in life, and then make a commitment to begin working on this *Right Now*. Working on this is not talking; it is taking action and following your path to success to the very end.

Do It Now

In the early parts of this book, I discussed putting your goals in writing and beginning to take action in the present moment. Hopefully you are well on your way with a plan in place and you have begun moving forward. If that is not the case then this is your reminder. Write your plan down *Now* and begin doing the appropriate research regarding your goal and putting it into action. I promise you that the Universe will be by your side once you start, but if you don't begin, there is no hope even for the Universe to help you. Do it *Now*.

58.

**If you want to make your dream come true the first thing you
have to do is wake up.**

J.M Power

It is never too late to begin or continue working on desires that you
have for yourself. Wake up and live your life rather than existing
in an imaginary world of stagnation and comfort. Do you want to
succeed? Do you want to escape the entrapment of the ordinary? Your
creator has nothing less planned for you than the extraordinary, but
remember, the Universe allows you to choose; you can either connect
to the flow of limitless and boundless energy or remain chained to
the limits and moronic demands of your animalistic ego.

Do It Now

Well, let's get on with it and begin taking steps to realize your
dreams. You must be cognizant of the fact that this eternal moment
belongs to you. What will you do with it? This decision is yours.
Don't procrastinate any longer.

59.

**To change ones life: Start immediately, do it flamboyantly,
no exception (no excuses).**
William James

There is no better time than right this moment to make changes in your life. Explore and venture out into the infinite domain of the Universe. There is always room for change and transformation in your life. Revolutionize your current way of living and marvel in the wonders of this exceptional opportunity to change *Right Now*. Make a decision to abandon your old way of thinking, believing, and living, and renovate your inner self. All of this is possible and starts with making a decision *Right Now* and following the guidance of the spectacular force, which awaits your companionship.

Do It Now

What do you desire to change in your life and how will you begin it *Right Now*? You can change anything you are determined and passionate about changing. Your opportunities for growth are limitless. Don't just read this, take my word for it, and put the book down. Write down the changes you wish to make and begin working on them. Desire, commitment and dedication are all that's needed in your personal transformation process.

60.
Listen closely... the present is calling you.
Richard A. Singer Jr.

If you permit your senses to escape the everyday chaos and confusion of society you will hear and feel the Universe gently calling you to join in and align yourself with the magnificent harmony of the present moment. There is no other moment like the one right in front of you. It is unique and filled with endless possibilities. You are completely free to do what you desire with each moment you are given.

Do It Now

Be creative *Now* at this very moment and do something unique, innovative, and completely spontaneous. What will you do? Surprise everyone. I can't wait to see what you choose.

61.

Wealth is the ability to fully experience life.

Henry David Thoreau

Take an adventure inside your heart today and seek what you sincerely value in your life. I am willing to anticipate that what you truly treasure is not money, power, fortune, or fame. Your heart almost certainly values other essential aspects of life such as love, respect, family, true friendship, and your children. The true definition of wealth is having an abundance of what you really value in your life and the ability to embrace and appreciate these gifts. Escape the deluded idea of wealth that most people cling to and truly assess your wealth based on what your heart and higher self values.

Do It Now

Make a commitment *Now* to continuously add to your true wealth and enjoy this each and every moment you are alive. Escape the misconception that wealth has to do with monetary and material possessions and then you will be alive experiencing the greatest gifts that life has to offer you.

62.
It is not the length of life, but depth of life.
Ralph Waldo Emerson

Forget about the past and don't worry about the future, just live deeply today. *Right Now* is all that life truly consists of. If you are not experiencing the present moment, you are not experiencing life. Throw yourself into the *Now* and experience the peace and serenity of living mindfully. Stop allowing life to pass you by and delight in it today. I believe this is where we will find genuine happiness. This is the secret of life. Living in the moment is the key to your success and tranquility that you have been searching external sources for way too long.

Do It Now

It is time to start experiencing life the way it was created to be. Live *Now* without projecting the useless past upon your current experience. When we project our past on the present, it creates a fog that obscures the joy and creation involved in the present moment. Each moment needs to be lived with clarity and complete innocence in order to experience the miracles that the *Now* contains.

63.

**If we really face up to things, we do not know which will
come first – tomorrow or death.**
His Holiness the Dalai Lama

Right here. Right Now. This very moment, filled with the loving
presence of the Universe, is all that you are truly guaranteed in
this life. Tomorrow, next week, even the next moment, may never
materialize. Create an exhilarating adventure right this instant; there
exists no future and no past. *Right Now* is all life is truly made of.

Do It Now

Picture yourself plummeting into the vast ocean of existence and
bathing in the soothing blue waters of the present moment. Become
fully awake and open to the sensations of the *Now*. *Right Now* is all
you have, just this single miraculous moment. You may be called to
return home at any time, so remind yourself that, "I am *Right Here,
Right Now*. The present moment is all that exists." You may want
to repeat this mantra to yourself to take full advantage of living
entirely in the *Now*. This may be your last moment, so make it a
special one.

64.
No valid plans for the future can be made by those who have no capacity for living now.
Alan Watts

People often view living in the *Now* as an idealistic but impractical way to live life. They perceive it as a possibility for "others", but definitely not for them. These people have too much to plan for, too much to think about, and too much to look forward to. Well I can certainly understand their thinking because this is what their ego desires for them to believe; and a powerful ego it is. However, I must say this pattern of thoughts and beliefs is entirely inaccurate. In reality, we are only guaranteed a great future by living a great *Now*. After all, what is the future? It's simply just another *Now* that we have yet to live. Combine and multiply great *Nows* and you get a great future.

Do It Now

Wake up and begin building the future you dream of right this second.

65.
Though no one can go back and make a brand new start, anyone can start from now and make a brand new ending.
Unknown Author

Each day brings a brand new lifetime to live. This life only lasts twenty-four hours and asks of you the best performance possible for this time period. Begin in this twenty-four-hour period to live according to your dreams and desires and commence living the life you were intended to live. It is never too late to change your direction in life and achieve what you imagined as an innocent child with idealism and wonder.

Do It Now

What do you want to be remembered for in this lifetime? What do you desire to leave the Universe when you transcend this part of your journey? These are questions that you must ponder. You can ponder them *Now*, or later. I assure you that *Now* is a better time because later will never come.

66.

**How wonderful it is that nobody need wait a single moment
before starting to improve the world.**
Anne Frank

Improving the world is a spiritual responsibility for every human being that inhabits the Universe. If we are not improving the world around us, then what are we doing here? The answer is either being inert or being destructive. Improvement of the world begins with one human being and blossoms across all of humanity. Advancement in humanity begins with the beliefs and dreams of one human being, which then transpires through united action among communities, societies, and eventually all cultures.

Do It Now

Make it your priority to begin doing something for the world today. If you are not doing something to improve the world then you are completely wasting your time. Choose something small and see how this small action makes an enormous difference. Never give up on making this world a better, more peaceful place.

67.

Live in the present as much as possible, past and future are merely thoughts, the present is life.

Dr. Richard Carlson

Our minds are great tools for life, although, when we live completely in our heads rather than living in life, we are unfortunately and unproductively misusing our cognitive faculties. The present is all that exists, all that is authentic, and it is all that can be changed. Many lives have been destroyed by the illusory thoughts of the past and future. From *Now* on, do not waste any more precious time, energy, or emotions on these delusions. Bask in the illumination and the bliss of the present and discover the enchantment and power of the *Now*.

Do It Now

Do not allow your thinking to lead you in an unproductive direction. Focus everything in the present and you become alive. Allow your thoughts to wander to the past or future and you will be caught in the delusions of your ego.

68.

To think too long about doing a thing often becomes its undoing.

Eva Young

Human beings are thinking animals and we often spend a majority of our time between our ears thinking away. However, life is also about doing and being. If we are trapped in the little circus in our heads for too long, we begin to lose consciousness of the outside world called "life". This constant obsessing and intellectualizing will drain you of life energy and keep you from enthusiastically living the life that your inner self desires. Do not get enthralled by the ego's intellectual demands and delusions. Step out of your cerebral playground and enjoy the wonders of the external Universe and all its jewels.

Do It Now

Do not allow yourself to become paralyzed by your neurotic and analytical mind. Begin doing, acting, being, and experiencing life to its fullest beyond your logical mind. You constantly think because you want control, but what has this brought you in the past. Relinquish this need for control and let the all-knowing Universe guide you along its natural course

69.

**Formulate and stamp indelibly on your mind a mental picture
of yourself as succeeding. Hold this picture tenaciously. Never
permit it to fade. Your mind will seek to develop the picture…
Do not build up obstacles in your imagination.**
Norman Vincent Peale

Whatever you truly believe deep within your being, and visualize
clearly within your soul, you will indeed accomplish. Never allow
negativity to impact your vision and always believe in yourself.
This picture of success that you invent will begin to transpire one
moment at a time if you continuously remain on your path and
apply tenacity and determination in every step of the process. The
cosmos will lend its power intimately to encourage you throughout
your journey.

Do It Now

What do you envision for your future and how will you begin acting
and programming yourself to achieve this dignified intention in
your life? Follow this formula and you will indeed be a complete
success in whatever area of your life that you are transforming.

70.

**Be content with the moment and be willing to follow the flow.
Then there will be no room for grief or joy. In the old days this
was called freedom from bondage.**

Chuang-Tzu

All our emotions, whether we judge them as good or bad, manifest
from our interpretations of life. We never really feel what it truly
is to be alive. We are always bound to what our egos allow us, and
make us, feel. Sometime our ego gives us a glimpse of joy; however,
for the majority of time, it leads us into intense mood swings, which
include grief, sadness, despair, regret and so on. Real joy is only
found in the tranquility and harmony of the present moment. Real
joy is the only genuine feeling that exists.

Do It Now

Begin to be aware and notice how the ego is involved in your
interpretation of life. Watch its tricks and manipulation, be aware of
its judgments and deceit, and know that the ego is not you. You are
the genuine part of your being that the ego is in conflict with. Clear
the debris of the ego and then you will know what is authentic in
life.

71.

**If you reflect on death and impermanence you will begin to
make your life meaningful.**
His Holiness the Dalai Lama

Each second of our life is so very valuable and fundamental in the
evolutionary process of our soul. If we begin to accept and embrace
our eventual departure from the physical world, we will come
to appreciate how sacred our lives actually are. There is indeed a
remote possibility that you won't be around to finish this book, say
the words I love you to a cherished family member, or see your
children advance in their lives. This is a reality that we often conceal
in the depths of our deluded ego. This armor of delusion keeps us
from truly valuing each present moment as the most divine aspect
we can experience in life.

Do It Now

Escape from behind the haze of misunderstanding and gently
surrender to the eternal present in your daily life. Start living each
moment of each day as if it was your last. Allow the spiritual gifts of
purpose, meaning, love and compassion to be the most vital areas
within your daily consciousness. Be right here, *Right Now* - just as
you are - and remember the impermanence of this physical life. You
will never again be blessed with a moment quite like this one.

72.

**The next time you're off to work, dreading the day ahead,
stop yourself.
Decide, just for one day, to think in a whole new way.**
Ben Stein

The process of change is initiated by doing things differently for just one day. It certainly cannot be harmful to decide today to do whatever it takes to discover some pleasure in work, to be creative, or to learn from those individuals around you that usually irritate you. Make a promise to yourself for just one day that you will feel the peace and joy of your capacity to actually be able to work and have a job. Keep in mind others throughout the world do not have the opportunity to even go to work or receive a paycheck. Some actually do not even eat on a regular basis or have clean water to drink. Be grateful today and change the way you perceive your life.

Do It Now

Make a decision to have a spectacular day today no matter what happens and you will experience how potent your mind is. Focus all your energy on this intention without allowing the distractions of your ego to overwhelm you. It's really simple, decide to do something and you will make it happen.

73.
Cease this very moment to identify yourself with the ego.
Shankara

Thoughts that manifest within your ego are not related to who you truly are. We are not our thoughts, we are not our ego, and we are not who society tells us we are. We are simply a reflection of the Soul of the Universe, which consists of the entirety of humanity. We are connected to everyone and everything that surrounds us. Once we realize this, we can begin to break through the illusion created by society and our ego, and only then can we enter the harmonious flow of energy that surrounds us.

Do It Now

Up until this very moment, you may have lived your life believing that you are what your ego identifies you as. This is a falsehood that must be corrected. You are a pure being that is one with all. To align with the Universal energy within you, you must slowly begin to detach from the fabricated-self that the ego has produced. When you begin to pull aside the veil of your ego, it is then that you discover the perfection that is present in the nucleus of your being. Take it slow, but begin to chip away at the membrane of delusion that your ego has preserved for way too long. *Right here, Right Now,* you are receiving the message to transcend the call of the ego and to fill yourself with spiritual energy.

74.

You are today where your thoughts have brought you; you will be tomorrow where your thoughts take you.

James Allen

This is an ideal time to pose a question to your inner self: Are you content today where your past thoughts have led you? If your answer is yes, wonderful. Continue to create the thoughts that take you where you truly desire to be. If your answer is no and you actually desire to be somewhere else, you need to change the way you think and behave in your life. Your transformation begins *Now*. Keep in mind that your thoughts and your beliefs are the building blocks and foundation of what you materialize in your external world.

Do It Now

Begin to think with the creativity and optimism that is innate within your being. Do not allow your ego to obscure the light that fills your natural being. When we think present-centered positive thoughts, we create results that align with our innate purpose and meaning in this life. When we think thoughts directed toward the past or future we are creating that which the ego desires.

75.
Not he who has much is rich, but he who gives much.
Erich Fromm

The yesteryears and the present moments illuminate the fact that those who are monetarily and materially rich can be very miserable, discontented, and severely depressed. In fact, some have actually chosen to end their lives. Take heed to this lesson and realize that material possessions and fortune do not do much for the soul. Giving makes the heart and soul grow and satisfies them more than any material thing can ever imagine. Do not rely on the destructive and deadly ego for the truth about reality; it will often lead you astray along a weary and ruinous journey.

Do It Now

Give something to someone else today. Rather than seeking, start incorporating giving in your daily life. This is how you will be fulfilled. The more you get, the more you want, and this never ends in satisfaction. However, give to one human being that is less fortunate than you, and satisfaction will permeate your entire being.

76.

First we form habits, then they form us. Conquer your bad habits, or they'll eventually conquer you.
Dr. Rob Gilbert

Think deeply and sincerely about the habits that you have formed throughout your life and how they dictate your behavior on a daily basis. Think carefully and choose one that you would like to make a commitment to change. It is important to list the pros and cons of continuing this habit, and then begin thinking about change, followed by making a firm decision and allegiance to take action one day at a time.

Do It Now

What habit will you begin to change *Now*? Take the time today to painstakingly contemplate if you truly want to change. If not, wait until later, the choice is yours and the rewards of change will be worth all the effort and sacrifice, but you must have a sincere desire to change. Good luck, but most importantly, do not give up on your determination and passion to change. Persistence, perseverance, and asking the Universal energy for help will get you through this major step one moment at a time. Changing your habits a little at a time will help you to embrace present-centered living.

77.

**The power of the present moment is so immense it is capable
– when lived in fully – of destroying forever every past
mistake and regret.**
Vernon Howard

The past in your life only exists if you create and believe your illusion that it exists. In reality, there is no past and traveling there to feel guilt over and over again is your choice. Why must you allow the unreal past to take peace and happiness away form your time in the present? Perhaps you feel unworthy of the gifts that are presented to you in the *Now*. Remember you choose between peace and guilt. It is not life or God or the Universe that desires this for you.

Do It Now

As we are approaching the conclusion of these reflections, I urge you to allow your ego to take you back to the past and appraise the things you consistently allow to obscure the present. Yes, I know you did this earlier in the book, however I know the ego and I am sure it is still holding on to past regrets. So once again, write these down, journal briefly about each one, share these things with someone you trust and ceremoniously destroy it by fire. Once you complete this process you must commit yourself to let go of all these burdens and completely give yourself to all that exists; the miraculous present that is accessible to all that yearn to be truly alive.

78.
The meaning in life is in all little things.
Zen Saying

Unfortunately, we allow the little things to pass us by while we are rushing around completing all of our never-ending futile tasks. We forget to cherish the smiles of our children, the beauty of a butterfly, or the magnificence of a sunset. The little things are what give us the most meaning and peace, yet we continue to allow them to pass us by while paying no attention whatsoever to them.

Do It Now

Begin noticing the meaning in all the little things in your life. Take a walk and feel the gratitude that you are healthy enough to actually walk and that you have the freedom to engage in the activities you desire. Gaze into the eyes of your loved ones and cherish the care and love that they provide you. Take some time to make a gratitude list of all the things you could not live without. Give more attention to these things daily and you will discover infinite meaning.

79.

A year from now you may wish you started from today.
Karen Lamb

We often reminisce about our past, and regret the things we did not accomplish that were passions and dreams belonging to us. We answer this regret with, "Well, it is too late now; I'll just get over it." Nevertheless, do you ever get over not fulfilling your innate desires and purpose? It is never too late to accomplish your dreams and fantasies. They need to be initiated *Right Now* without turning back. You owe this to yourself and the Universe. Get to work and begin creating what you truly desire. This is what life is all about; don't let it slip away again because you may not have the opportunity to pursue your dreams in the future.

Do It Now

Take a step toward fulfilling one of your soul's burning desires. It is never too late to accomplish what you were meant to accomplish. It is not that difficult, once you put your dream into action, the momentum of the Universe will be with you all the way. It will guide you to your desires realization.

80.

Words!
The Way is beyond language
For in it there is,
No yesterday
No tomorrow
No today.
Seng-Ts'an

Words are potent, yet they can never capture the true essence and splendor of reality. We use them because we must, but never believe that they paint an accurate picture of life. All words limit our perception and our internal power to experience what the Universe actually holds for us. When we can just *Be* then we will truly *See* what is available in the *Now*. This is Truth and Beauty. This is Enlightenment!

Do It Now

At this very moment let your entire organism simply *Be*. Notice the feelings, let your thoughts drift away, let go of the illusory words that come to your mind and allow yourself to be embraced in the arms of Truth. This takes practice so don't renounce it before you have the chance to experience the endless and eternal sea of Being.

81.

We cannot put off living until we are ready. The most salient characteristic of life is its urgency, "here and now" without any possible postponement. Life is fired at us point blank.

Jose Ortega y Gasset

If you follow the weary path that the ego sets out before you, readiness for genuinely living will be swallowed up, and you will never be given the opportunity to experience the life that awaits you by living completely in the present. Yes, your decision is urgent because reality waits for no one. The *Here and Now* is life, but our ego's goal is to take this away from us by demanding that we live elsewhere. You must abandon this path.

Do It Now

There is no time to wait. The splendor and serenity of life awaits you and you must make a decision right this moment to bring yourself back to the *Now* and align with the vigorous flow of the Universe. This involves progress not perfection. One moment at a time, you can begin releasing yourself from the bondage of the past and future and accept that all that is, and will ever be, is eternal presence.

82.

If you really want to get to the truth of Zen, get it while walking, while standing, while sleeping or sitting...while working.
Pen-Hsien

When we focus completely on the moment and are mindful of the task at hand we allow ourselves to *Be* and escape the chains of the egocentric facet of our minds. We give ourselves to the authenticity of life and allow ourselves to experience each task as miraculous. Rather then giving into the robotic nature of society and rushing through everything in front of us to actually go nowhere, we experience all that we are and all that the Universe has to offer us.

Do It Now

Become one with each activity you are engaged in. That's all, it's that simple.

83.

One of the most tragic things I know about human nature is that all of us tend to put off living.
Dale Carnegie

Life is a playground of endless opportunities for improvement, peace, and genuine satisfaction. There are so many precious moments to experience, opportunities for growth, and dreams to be materialized. The Universe wants nothing less than for you to bathe in the experience and joy of life's journey. Do not put off the opportunity to play, and enjoy the pleasures of a truly fulfilled experience that is available for you throughout each moment of everyday. Go and play, enjoy, and dance in the ecstasy of life.

Do It Now

Continue pursuing the unfilled dreams and desires you have thought about previously while reading this book. Be sure you are keeping on track and not putting off what you really need to accomplish in life. At times, the capitalistic chaos will knock you off track and push you to seek what you do not really need. Simply be mindful of this, and pick yourself up and continue following what you really know your true desires to be.

84.

The future depends on what we do in the present.

Gandhi

What you do in each moment ultimately adds up to be your future. There is no reason to worry or fret about the future because you have control of what you do with each moment you live today. Create the best moments you possibly can and your future will consist of all that you desire. Discontinue your habitual need to pollute the present with regret and guilt from the past and constant worries about the future. Center yourself and exude excellence in the *Now* and the future you desire will take care of itself.

Do It Now

Focus all of your thoughts and energy in the present moment and begin orchestrating the future that belongs to you. You can be sure if you live in the past and project yourself into the future you will never have what you desire.

85.

Forever is composed of Nows.

Emily Dickinson

These five simple words completely summarize what life is all about. We often falsely perceive what forever means, but if we truly look at life as it genuinely is, we discover that forever does not really exist. Reality is timeless and only consists of the *Now*. Wherever you are, it will always be *Right Now*. Don't believe for a second that you have forever to begin living your life.

Do It Now

Right Now is all you will ever have. You will never know when your time will be up. At some present moment, it will be time for you to leave this earth and then you will wish that you had made the most of the *Nows* that you were so freely given. Decide what is most important and precious to you and embrace it while you still have the time.

86.

**It is characteristic of the ego that it takes all that is unimportant
as important and all that is important as unimportant.**
Meher Baba

Let's see how this deceptive mechanism of the ego works. What
does the ego think is important? Most of the time its material things,
money, property, prestige, being different from everyone, belittling
people, judging people and separating humans based on external
traits. What does it see as unimportant? Most of the time family is
put near the bottom of our list of priorities. Other things that the ego
makes unimportant include equality, joy, genuine care for humanity,
and peace.

Do It Now

Sit down right this moment and make a list of what is really
important to you. If you were lying on your death bed, what would
you wish you did more of? If you were to find out you would die
tomorrow what would you do right at this moment? Do it *Now* and
begin living based on what is genuinely important to your being
and not your ego.

87.

We must use all opportunities to practice the truth, to improve ourselves instead of waiting for a time we think we will be less busy.
His Holiness the Dalai Lama

If you are like the majority of human beings on this earth you rush from one place to the next not noticing anything in your path. You multi-task not putting any passion into what you do and you continue this pace each and every day. When your restful vacation comes, you can't sit still for a moment because your habitual, monotonous, daily behavior has taken over all your humanity. Is this Truth, or life, or even enjoyable at all?

Do It Now

Slow the hell down! Excuse my language, but get a life. Step out of the rat race led by society and begin searching within to discover the being you are. You are not a tool for society to use. You are a human being that needs to seek meaning, experience the miraculous, and grow in order to help heal and transform the world. Focus on your real purpose and seek the Truth. I guarantee you the Universe was not created for you to run around like a useless android.

88.

We are all affecting the world every moment, whether we mean to or not. Our actions and states of mind matter, because we are so deeply connected with one another.
Ram Dass

This deep connectedness of all livings things, this Truth, has been lost because of human beings need to be separate and be different from each other. This is one of the faultiest concepts humans have devised. We have separated the human race into distinct groups based on exterior characteristics such as color, language, ethnicity, etc. To separate based on these things is one of the most immature ways of thinking there is. The Universe very simply demonstrates that we are all equal and all belong to one another.

Do It Now

Just a simple change in our thinking can transform the world. It's as simple as practicing the truth of equality. There is actually no way to dispute this simple Universal fact. Begin practicing equality as your little way to transform humanity.

89.

True Patience – A non-grasping openness to
whatever comes next.
Stephen Levine

Patience is a quality that is indispensable when living in the present moment. We must accept and cherish what comes and goes without attempting to control or manipulate the truth. Whenever we reach into life and try to make it the way we want it or think it should be, we really are destroying it and causing unnecessary tension and grief within ourselves. To be free is to enter the flow of life and ride the smooth but powerful wave of acceptance.

Do It Now

Let peace and serenity freely enter your life without barricading it with your ego. This truly does not take any effort. You just let it be and your internal rewards will come. This is effortless. Relax and just be and you will soon see what I am talking about. Try it, it won't hurt.

90.

**Impermanence is a principle of harmony. When we don't
struggle against it, we are in harmony with reality.**
Pema Chodron

We know from the scientific study of the human being that at no
moment in life do our bodies remain the same. We are constantly
changing just as everything in the Universe is in constant flux.
Nothing, absolutely nothing will remain the same from moment to
moment. This is a fact we must begin to integrate in our lives. We
cannot stop change, thus we must adapt and accept the change in
our lives. To continue your efforts to control and stop the momentum
and natural flow of the Universe will always give you nothing but
conflict and anguish.

Do It Now

You must completely come to acceptance with reality. Hop on the raft
of life and peacefully float along the wondrous river of the Universe.
Accepting change and becoming one with the natural momentum
will allow you to experience the miraculous and beauty of all things.
This can only be accomplished through your consistent practice of
mindfulness. Remember mindfulness is simply being aware of the
Nowness of life.

91.

**To be free of all authority, of your own and that of another, is
to die to everything of yesterday, so your mind is always fresh,
always young, innocent, full of vigor and passion.**

J. Krishnamurti

All the egos of the world seek one thing, and one thing only, and that
is to have control and power over human beings. Your ego wants
control and complete dominion over you and anyone else that will
succumb to its illusive power. This ego has developed throughout
time and keeps gaining strength because we continue to feed it and
nurture it. The only time in your life that you were not under its
control was when you were an innocent little boy or girl, living
adventurously and spontaneously. It's been a long time since you
were free.

Do It Now

The essence of any spiritual practice is to return to the innocence
and freedom of childhood. Begin to go back and play freely with
passion and see the miracles in everything like it was the first time
you are experiencing it. You can play, dance and sing anytime you
choose.

92.

You see we are all dying. It's only a matter of time. Some of us just die sooner than others.
Dudjom Rinpoche

Our idea of death and confrontation of its reality can actually motivate us to truly live rather than walking around as if we are dead. Living completely by your ego and going along in life according to the monotonous activities of society, is merely existing, which is as if we were actually dead. This is no way to live if you want to truly embrace what life has to offer. Living is being completely in the present moment, which opens you up to the spontaneous and adventurous qualities of life. Wake up and live.

Do It Now

Be brutally honest with yourself when answering this next question. Are you freely living an adventure, or are you existing bound to the ideas of your ego and society? Only you have the answer and only you have the key to escape this dreary and dreadful path of existence.

93.
Tomorrow isn't promised to anyone.
Walter Payton

We must sit down and honestly assess whether we are living in the *Now*, in the past, or in the future. Do you have great plans for tomorrow? Well you might as well dispose of them because tomorrow never comes. The plans you make must begin *Now*. This illusion of the future and the past has taken way too much away from you. It is now time to accept the truth and live realistically. I have said it many times, but I will repeat it once more. All you possess and will ever possess is *Right Now*. Make use of this moment that has been given to you and join the euphoria of life.

Do It Now

We are nearing the end of our journey together. At this point, I hope you are allowing the Truth to enter your being and whole-heartedly recognizing that there is nothing real except the *Now*. If you are still questioning this reality, you are still allowing your ego to deceive you. No one but you can allow this punishment to continue. Do you enjoy your suffering? If not then why are you making life so difficult?

94.

**When you were born, you cried and the world rejoiced.
Live your life in such a manner that when you die the world
cries and you rejoice.**
Indian Saying

The distinction that we draw between life and death is certainly not
based on reality. It's simply a product of our conditioning in this
world. Life and death do not oppose each other, but are unified. Death
is purely another moment or aspect of our soul's eternal journey. We
must fully accept death before we can actually live life. Embrace and
welcome the opportunity to transition to another dimension of life.
There is no need to fill yourself with fear or dread. The world may
be sad because the physical *you* has departed; however, I urge you
to enter the temple of death with an open heart, for you cannot even
begin to imagine what is in store for you.

Do It Now

Develop your plan for truly living during the remaining time of
your life. Keep focused on your new *Living Plan* because this is all
that exists; death is simply entering another phase of our existence.
What do you plan to bequeath to this world when it is time to move
on? What do you wish to complete before you leave? These are the
existential questions to focus on. When you have written out your
personalized *Living Plan*, it is then time to get to work. Remember,
you don't know if you will be in this realm for decades, years,
months, days, or a few more moments. Get to work on your plan
Now, and don't let up

95.

There is nothing that wastes body like worry, and one who has any faith in God should be ashamed to worry about anything whatsoever.
Gandhi

It has been scientifically confirmed that worry eats away at your body, your mind, and of course your soul. In addition to this, it is obvious that worry is the most unproductive task we can ever engage ourselves in. It takes us away from life, causes intense stress, and solves absolutely nothing. Why do you insist on doing it so often?

Do It Now

Do you like to harm yourself, engage in useless thinking, and cause intense anxiety for no apparent reason? Would you go outside your house and begin digging a hole for no apparent reason, and continue for no apparent reason, until eventually you collapse in exhaustion? Of course you wouldn't, so why do you worry? Stop the worrying this moment. It is not an innate part of us, it is a learned behavior that the ego adopted to destroy all peace and serenity in your life.

96.
Simplicity is the most difficult of all things.
Swami Ajaya, PhD

The path to enlightenment lies in realizing that the essence of life is simplicity and we must practice this philosophy in each precious moment we are blessed to experience. This is where bliss is discovered. Unfortunately, most human beings will question this viewpoint and continue on with the persistent intellectualization and over complication of life. This is okay too, but prior to deciding which road to travel, one must obtain experiential knowledge of both paths. To condemn any path without direct experience and observation is to live a life of ignorance. You may be condemning the very thing that will liberate you from your anguish.

Do It Now

Dedicate one day in your life to live completely in the moment, accepting all that flows in through your daily experience. Live simply, and from your soul. Allow the all-encompassing energy of the Universe to carry you in its flowing perfection of simplicity and bliss. Allow all thoughts and intellectualizations to come and go like the passing clouds. Live in the *Now* and simply be you, right here with nowhere to run and nowhere to hide. Just you and the moment, enjoying the intimacy of life.

97.

Wanting is seeking elsewhere. Completeness is being right here.
Stephen Levine

Within the psyche of a majority of human beings is the myth created by the capitalistic system that we need more and more and more, ad infinitum. We supposedly need these things to be content, accepted, and victorious. Unfortunately, this is your manipulative ego at work setting you on an endless journey that will never cease. The only thing you truthfully need is to accept and be joyful with what you have.

Do It Now

Look in front of you, around you and within you, and realize that you are whole. Stop this endless journey of desire, and enjoy the happiness you already possess. Cherish the love and light that exists and share it with your family, friends, and all of humanity. Take a look at your past wants that you have successfully grasped and the achievements you have amassed. Did these complete you like you once thought, or have you created more desires to chase after?

98.

**Life is a series of natural and spontaneous changes.
Don't resist them—that only creates sorrow. Let reality be reality.
Let things flow naturally forward in whatever way they like.**
Lao Tzu

No matter how hard you try, or the illusions of control you hold onto, you will never be able to make life or reality do what you personally wish. The fact remains that reality is reality and the only cure to this is acceptance of what is. Of course you can bang your head over and over against this concrete wall of illusion, however, the best result you are going to get is a tremendous headache filled with the wonders of anxiety, grief, and helplessness. So, as it stands, would you like peace or constant turmoil?

Do It Now

Just for this moment simply commit yourself to the flow of life without the ego's resistance. Practice acceptance for all that comes your way. An old saying that comes to mind that literally saved my life in the early stages of my recovery from addiction and keeps me grounded in the present is as follows:

"Acceptance is the answer to all my problems today. When I am disturbed, it is because I find some person, place, thing – some fact of my life – unacceptable to me, and I can find no serenity until I accept that person, place, thing or situation as being exactly the way it is supposed to be at this moment" (Alcoholic Anonymous Text, pg. 449).

Listen to the profound wisdom in this passage and practice it mindfully today. Experience how you feel and then you can choose between acceptance and resistance.

99.

An adult is one who has lost the grace, the freshness, the innocence of the child, who is no longer capable of feeling pure joy, who makes everything complicated, who spreads suffering everywhere, who is afraid of being happy, and who, when everything goes better, goes back to sleep.
The wise man is a happy child.
Arnaud Desjardins

As we come to the end of the meditations and enter the next part of this book, I dare you to become an innocent and happy child. Go forth in your life, feeling joyous, spreading peace, and living freely each precious moment that you are given. Let your soul experience the freedom of life and most of all do not waste anymore time living in the confines created by your ego.

Do It Now

I challenge you to live according to the Ultimate flow of life and enjoy all the gifts that are available in each moment of your precious existence. I must thank you for joining me in the first part of this book and allowing my words to enter your being. It is now time to be inspired by incredible human beings who contributed heart-filled essays to help you practice staying in the *Now* in your life. These passionate words will surely prove to you that present centered living is possible and actually the only way to truly live a fulfilling and peaceful life.

Part II

Is it Possible to Live in the Now?

Losing My Mind To Come To My Senses
Edie Weinstein

As I am typing these words, my body; this vehicle that totes around my essence is sitting in half lotus with the laptop in front of me on the purple cotton sheets of my bed, mounds of pillows support my back. It is a glorious, sun splashed Sunday morning. Music is sweetly issuing forth from my radio; the sounds of my favorite weekend morning show called Sleepy Hollow on WXPN 88.5 in Philadelphia. On my bedside table, a cup of ginger tea beckons and I sip in between words. What a juxtaposition of images and experiences. Input from all directions. Present and not present all at once.

Memory of a joyful occasion yesterday, floats into my awareness. The wedding of friends held at an exquisite retreat center called Mt. Eden Retreat where kindred spirits gathered to celebrate the joining of this lovely couple. Love, laughter, luscious pot luck food, delightful dancing, heart opening conversation; is there much better than that? As my physical container is here and now, my mind, sometimes my friend, sometimes my adversary is off a full day ago, having its way. This time it is a pleasant encounter with the 'past'. On other occasions, not so delightful as all of the 'shoulda, woulda, coulda' thoughts come flooding back. Monkey mind chatter that plagues me with fear, lack and limitation. When able, I feed the monkey a virtual banana to quiet her for a bit. The question is: Is either one of these mental meanderings 'real' once the event has passed?

As I allow for the pleasurable experiences from yesterday to flow through, my body recalls it as if it is happening in the moment; with cellular memory kicking in and I smile. As I permit the erstwhile 'yucky' thoughts to hold sway, my throat tightens, my belly knots up and I feel lightheaded. My body doesn't know the difference, but my conscious, awakening mind and heart can tell and it is at that point that I can question what is 'real'. And so my day goes, wavering back and forth between those two states. Pain and pleasure. Truth and fallacy. I choose in which to remain. Awareness is the key. So much is under the surface and when I am in the moment, I can tell the difference.

One of my many hats is that of a journalist who, for the past 20-some years has interviewed many of the best known wisdom teachers on the planet; from His Holiness the Dalai Lama, to Ben and Jerry. One of my favorites is Dan Millman; author of "Way of The Peaceful Warrior". A line from the book that stands out for me is this one: "Sometimes you have to lose your mind to come to your senses." In modern culture, the concept of losing our minds is terrifying. Another of my guises is that of a social worker in a psychiatric hospital, so that particular reference is pejorative. When I consider the loss of mind, I sometimes smile since at times, my mind is like a small child behind the wheel of a runaway bus on a collision course with a brick wall. She is having a blast, even though she can't quite see over the steering wheel. I gotta get the adult to commandeer the bus while encouraging the child to learn how to responsibly drive. Not always an easy task but necessary if I am to live effectively in the world.

A few years ago, I heard Dan Millman speak and he shared a story about an encounter he had with a man who had come to one of his presentations. After that event, Dan was standing around, casually in conversation with audience members and the man approached him with a request. He said something to the effect of "I know you probably get paid a lot of money for your time, but I only have a dollar and I wanted a piece of wisdom." Dan holds out his hand, the man places the dollar in it and steps back to wait. Dan looks the man in the eye and says "Here and now. Breathe and relax." Six simple, but ultimately profound words. That, to me, is the essence of mindfulness.

As much of a consummate multi-tasker as I have become, I still need to be conscious and aware of what I do. Purposeful Zen in action. I walk in my front door and place my keys on my dresser so I know where they will be when I need them again. I methodically kick off my shoes and put them away in the closet. When I get in the car, I take a deep breath before pulling out of the driveway and remind myself where I am going and consider how I will get there (of course, the GPS helps). When I am about to enter an interaction with anyone, whether joyfully anticipating or dreading, I take another inhale and exhale and ask that it be for the highest good, regardless of outcome. Each of these behaviors take but a moment and yet are ultimately priceless since they make my life richer.

Other techniques I use that keep me grounded and centered in the present:

Heartbeat Living
I place one hand on my heart and the other on my abdomen, taking deep belly breaths and really feeling the physical being. I sense my heart beating and know that I am alive and in the moment.

Yoga Off The Mat
I practice yoga, consciously aware of each movement, taking time to slow each posture. That was not always the case, since as a recovering Type A, I was in competition with myself to stretch farther and hold a pose longer, just to prove I could. I take this off the mat and into my daily life, going to my edge and only a wee bit further, as singer songwriter Karen Drucker eloquently shares "I will only go as fast as the slowest part of me feels safe to go."

Divine Dishwashing
When I do dishes, I allow for indulging in the feeling of the warm, soapy water on my hands, so that it doesn't seem like an arduous task. Afterward, I feel a sense of accomplishment, when I see clean dishes.

Sweet Treats
More often than not lately, I have been mindfully eating. With my

busy schedule, too often, I have rushed through meals. When it is something I particularly enjoy, like ice cream, I become a hedonist. Yesterday, I had a coconut ice cream cone and immersed in all of the sensual pleasures contained in that sweet treat as I walked down the street of one of my favorite towns of New Hope, PA, taking in the sights, sounds and smells.

Full Presence

Being present with people in my life. Before my husband died more than 11 years ago, I had an encounter with the Divine that I call "God wrestling". I emphatically told the Creator: "He's mine and you can't have him." and the loving and equally emphatic response was "He's mine and he's on loan to you, like everyone else in your life." A singer-songwriter friend named Charley Thweatt has a song called "You Will Die Someday". Two of the most poignant lines are "Take your time when you're being with people. What's another minute to you?" which remind me that I need not rush through talking with anyone. That additional time with them may make all the difference in the world for both of us.

And so, off into my day, with heart open and mind lost and gained all at once.

About the Author

Rev. Edie Weinstein, MSW, LSW is a Renaissance Woman and Bliss Mistress who delights in inviting people to live rich, full, juicy lives. Her business is called By Divine Design, the title of which came to her in a dream. Edie is an internationally recognized, sought after, colorfully creative journalist, interviewer and author, a dynamic and inspiring speaker, licensed social worker and interfaith minister, offering uniquely designed spiritual rituals. She is currently writing her first best seller: The Bliss Mistress Guide To Transforming The Ordinary Into The Extraordinary. To find out more about Edie visit her website at www.liveinjoy.org.

Live Your Own Life
Stephanie Mansour

Throughout my life, I've heard many of my friends and family say, "I need to stay at this job (that I hate, that isn't right for me, insert reason why you don't want to be HERE) for at least 2 years to look credible." or "You need to stick out this job you hate because XYZ (insert fearful reason HERE).

Thankfully, I never listened to any of this advice! After graduating college, I took a job in New York. After a month, I realized this was not what I wanted to be spending 50 hours a week doing! Feeling totally lost and upset, I was randomly offered an amazing job on the west coast - the only problem was I had 7 days to quit my job in New York, sublet my apartment, move out to Los Angeles, and start my new job. All of these obstacles did not seem like difficulties at the time. While some people thought I was crazy, I knew that I was working a job I hated, and wanted something new. Why should I spend my time, in the present, doing something I hated, for a second longer?

I began working at my new job in Los Angeles, and 9 months in I was again feeling like this wasn't the right place for me. My parents thought I was crazy when I refused the potential offer of doubling my salary and a promotion, but deep down I knew this wasn't the job for me. Against the advice of my parents and bosses, I decided to leave my job after 9 months, without a plan.

I started doing more yoga, used breathing techniques, and tried meditation in order to become more mindful and decide what exactly I wanted to do with my life. With funds running out, I decided to take a desk job (that I hated from day 1!) just to pay the bills. I pursued my passions on the side, and thankfully was laid off after 6 months of work.

Knowing that I was being kicked in the behind and forced to dive in to my real mission, the day I was laid off I started my company, Step It Up with Steph. I knew that there was no day but today, and that if I didn't start my company that day, I wouldn't start it. I totally embraced my new found job and hit the ground running. I also felt that the best way to grow my company was to move back to the Midwest, where I am from. So I packed up and moved to Chicago, my third city in 3 years. Currently I am the happiest I have ever been, surrounded by my friends and doing what I love.

Throughout the development of my company, I've learned even more about the importance of tuning in and listening to my gut, my core, and what my deepest self really wants. While it is very easy to get caught up in forward thinking, fear-based reasons why I shouldn't do something, and "buts", I always try to keep in mind that the only way I've gotten to where I am today is by being more mindful and living in the *NOW*. By focusing on what is happening and what I am feeling right now, I have created Step It Up with Steph and am creating my ultimate dream: my Health & Fitness TV Show.

About the Author

Stephanie Mansour is a Health & Fitness Expert and Body Image Coach. She also trains private clients in Chicago and does health & fitness TV segments. For more information about Steph visit her at www. StepItUpwithSteph.com

Grandma's Kitchen
Sherry Jones Mayo

People who spend their lives working in Emergency Services tend to develop a strong stomach, incredibly insane sense of humor, and a network that keeps them resilient in the most bizarre (or emotionally painful) circumstances. Those whose duties revolve around what people should not do or see need a way to survive, a solid foundation, and an unwavering support system to keep unpleasant experiences from invading their peace and damaging their spirit. For me, survival is playing with my kitten Izzy, burying my face in my husband's chest, breathing deeply to inhale the sense of calm that he brings, or going back to my roots.

My mother was born in this country, but my grandparents were not. Grandpa and Grandma brought with them, from Moro D'Oro, Italy, a rich cultural heritage that stressed famiglia (family) as the center of the universe. Family-centered living is a lesson I have passed on to my own children. My mother never knew her grandparents, and I am grateful to have known mine, as Grandpa and Grandma certainly helped mold me into the person I am today, influencing as well the adults my children have become.

No one in the family ever had much money, which is a good thing. We inherited a sense of duty, ethics, and hard work, not one of privilege or entitlement. With a downwardly spiraling economy, I have found that now more than ever I rely on family as the center of my world, and the teachings of my parents and grandparents still guide me. I have learned many lessons, among them that if you want something, you work for it. If you want respect, you earn it. Happiness is now, not, "I will be happy when ..." And if you want to have a safe, warm, and loving place to go when life gets tough, you go to Grandma's Kitchen.

Grandma's wishes always superseded Mama's rules -- one way we honored the little Italian woman who, in her adulthood, called

America home. Mama acquiesced gratefully, knowing that the treasures and lessons that filled her own childhood would find their way into our young lives.

The center of Gram's universe was her kitchen. She was a tiny woman at 4'8", further dwarfed by her kitchen, the most expansive area in the house. We all gathered in that kitchen and laughter echoed from every corner, reverberating with the sunlight off the thinly painted pale, block walls, and bare cement floor. Grandma was constantly laughing, so filled with the purest joy of being alive and happily surrounded by her children and grandchildren.

Joys, sorrows, accomplishments, and challenges came to Grandma's kitchen for celebration or consolation, so Gram was continually feeding our stomachs and our souls. The largest pots, for spaghetti and sauce, were always in use. Sauce bubbled merrily, sometimes escaping the confines of the pot and dancing onto the white ceramic stovetop with varying patterns of rich, dark red artistry. The saucepot never stood too long before someone came along and gave it a good stir with the ever-present large, wooden spoon, aged well and darkened with the richness of home grown Roma tomatoes. Following the stirring, one was entitled to a quick taste, and a hunk of hard-crust bread slipped into the pot, almost accepting the dipper's fingertips. No one dared, after consuming the bit of bread, to suggest adding anything more to the mixture. The sauce was always perfect, made with pork and beef slices that cooked until they nearly melted, as was the Abruzzi region custom.

Pasta joined the sauce many hours later, but the time was not wasted. We never knew boredom, because Grandma taught us the most important moment was the one you were in, and made sure to fill each second with life through busy hands: make a pot of coffee, shell nuts, wash and chop the fruits and vegetables waiting their turn on the farm-style kitchen table. Gram made her own pasta, deftly stretching it out with a converted broomstick handle used as a rolling pin on that massive tabletop standing in the center of her kitchen.

We always sat nearby, learning cooking secrets passed through generations but never written, knowing that measurements were subjective; taste, smell, and color told all. We nibbled on treats as Gram cooked; her familiar appeal in a thick Italian accent to, "Yeat, yeat -- you too skinny, you get sick" melodically ringing in our ears as she delivered it with love and laughter. Gram would wipe her hands on a blue-flowered handmade apron, and pat our heads and shoulders as she laughed gleefully at our enjoyment of the items she proffered. I never decided which was better, the food, or the delight on Gram's face as she watched us consume it. In either case, it was obviously a labor of love, and I wish I had spent more time living in those moments than later trying to remember them.

In my adult world, a place in which things constantly go bump in the night, the unexpected can cause a shift in worldviews formerly thought as firmly cemented. The only way to live peacefully is in the present because one truly has no concept of what may happen a minute from now. If life is constantly focused on the destination, the journey is lost; enjoying the moment becomes too foreign a concept to appreciate, and running and reaching for expectations depletes a soul of the fuel it needs to get to the next moment, or to enjoy the 'now' experience. Unmet expectations increase anxiety, and living a life of lists and demands is far from peaceful.

I lived that life, striving for the future, working on goals (short-term, long-term, and adapting to new circumstances) until a high-speed rollover forced instant introspection. Maybe life-threatening or life-changing experiences are necessary for over-achievers who measure life's value in concrete results (reaching personal, educational, and professional goals). Maybe our time-space continuum has to experience a violent shift to realize we are running to stay still. Accepting a world that focuses on future items distracts us until we, under duress, re-examine the value of our lives and contributions, possibly revealing that we may have missed what was genuinely important along our journey.

As a Paramedic RN with over 20 years in emergency services

and almost as many years as a crisis responder, I see folks in pain, experiencing unexpected loss and major life changes. When I teach courses in crisis management, I like to share a simple lesson my Aunt Mary Jo, Grandma's youngest daughter, taught many years ago: always part with "I love you." End every conversation, whether on the phone, in an e-mail, or with a hug at the door as your family member is leaving, with those three words, and you will never have to worry or wonder about the last thing you said if something happens. Aunt Mary Jo's tradition reinforced that we do not know what tomorrow brings, so live completely in today. I lost Auntie Mary Jo, her husband Tad, and my Dad in a six-month period. Working through pain and loss, I knew one thing: my last words to each were, "I love you." Awareness of every moment gives one a tremendous sense of peace, as no one knows when the next moment may change life forever.

Gram's colander, apron, and rolling pin reside with me. I have none of her cooking recipes, but her recipe for a simple, happy life lives deeply within my heart, and I mentally go back to her kitchen at will. I can close my eyes and see the rows of baking supplies, home-canned goods, and staples on the shelves of her pantry, smell the pasta, sauce, and fresh bread, and hear her laughter. I hope someday my grandchildren will find a haven and a big helping of fond memories in my kitchen, too. What I can give them now as they and their children grow is an appreciation for this moment, a sense of journey rather than future and goals. I can teach them that this moment is exactly as it should be. Then I can make them spaghetti.

About the Author

Sherry Jones Mayo is a native of Michigan, a registered nurse, and a licensed paramedic. She has over two decades of experience in emergency medicine, including 14 years as a trauma nurse. Combining her experience in emergency medicine and critical incident stress management (CISM) with a love for writing, Sherry has published in several military, civilian, medical, collegiate, and internet forums. Sherry is a member of, and Approved Instructor for the International Critical Incident Stress Foundation (ICISF). She is also a Diplomate with the American Academy of Experts in Traumatic Stress. Sherry lives in Sedona, Arizona with her husband Gary and their four-footed son, Izzy. To find out more about Sherry visit her website at www.SherryJonesMayo.com.

Kite Tail Tales
Cathy Runyan Svacina

Years ago I designed the best watch in the world. It is more accurate than any atomic clock. It requires no batteries. It automatically adjusts instantly to any time zone, and if you look closely at the clock face, you will see just one word... *Now*!

And if you walk into my underground home from the above- the -ground garage, you will have a choice to make. You can either walk down the eighteen steps or you can choose to go down the big slide into the bean bag! Either way, if you look up at the blue and white cloud painted sky ceiling, you will see a kite with a very long tail.

Now, how do these odd things all connect? Thirty years ago, I could not answer that.

Now, I can. Every morning when I wake up, I am excited about the possibilities of the day. I am excited about the things I may learn, the ways I may grow, the people I may help... all because I try to stay open to the moment... each moment.

Visualize a kite with me. Give it a very long tail. Now start tying scrap rags onto the tail. Notice how very few of them match? Some may blend, but many may clash. That's not only *ok*, but it's great! There are polka dots, stripes, plaids and swirls. There are flowers and plain solids and denims and silks. Very few of those rags tied onto the tail really look like they go together, but take that kite out to fly and what will you see? You will see how all of those different "rag life experiences" on the kite's tail *are* connected and work together to actually help balance and guide the flight of that kite.

When people bypass daily *Now* opportunities to learn, to grow, to share, to love, to feel or to experience life in any positive way because it doesn't seem to match with their career or social paths, then they are often choosing to lose out on valuable moments. Moments that in the end, could improve the balance and direction of their life kites! To pass up polka dot experiences because they don't match your striped experiences, may eventually lead to regrets. Each night when I am able to put my head down on my pillow and have no regrets for that day is in itself a wonderful joyful moment. With that in mind, I consciously make decisions throughout the day to avoid regrets later.

For example, once when our little town of Parkville, Missouri was hosting the reenactment of the Lewis and Clark Discovery ship voyage on the Missouri River, the Captain invited me to join the crew for one day. I had about 60 seconds to make my decision before they pushed off from the shore. With no cell phone around, I grabbed my business card out of my purse, and turned to a woman walking by and asked her to please call my husband and tell him I would call that night when we landed at the next scheduled town. Thank goodness, I knew my husband would understand.

No way did I want to someday be sitting in a rocking chair and thinking, "Why didn't I take that Captain up on his generous offer to let me be part of the crew for one day?" No way did I want to miss an opportunity to have a wonderful new life experience or to learn something I didn't know or a chance to make new friends. Going for the *Now* moment, I jumped on that boat just as they were pushing off, and I did have an incredible day and evening on the Missouri River with the Lewis and Clark crew. One particular memory from that trip has been a source of inspiration and energy for me on several occasions since then. I was taking my turn on the front of the ship watching for debris from the recent floods and signaling the captain to steer to the left or the right. I laughed when they tied my ankle to a rope just in case we hit some hidden debris and I was knocked off the boat. But while I was on duty, I saw in the distance an odd log with branches that seemed to be moving against the current. As we got closer, I was able to see that it was a deer trying to swim across the river and incredibly, in his antlers was a small squirrel clinging on for "deer" life. I signaled the crew to come and look. Together we all anxiously watched the struggling deer in the strong current, but when it finally made it to the shore safely, along with his squirrel passenger, we all broke into spontaneous cheering. That experience alone taught me much about supporting and helping others, and the importance of perseverance and never giving up. I gave that unique experience a rare paisley rag on my life's kite tail.

I have also learned that with daily practice, our brains can learn to sort between the pros and cons of decisions with computer like speed. And maybe it is not so much a matter of practice as of giving yourself permission to go with both the spiritual intuition that can often follow our brain's analysis of a situation and your own gut feeling, versus our somewhat inept intellectual approach. I believe when we allow for it, our brains and our spirits are capable of achieving a much greater accuracy of the positive or negative potential of decisions we make as compared to just depending solely on our intellectual reasoning. But it is imperative for me to explain that I also believe in a power much greater than myself and this belief in God not only energizes me, but also brightens my attitude every day. It is partly because of this belief that I am able to be at peace with living in the moment and not worrying about the future other than to do what I can *Now* to prepare myself as best I can for the future by living a life free of regrets.

And how often did I wake up my sleeping children and carry them out to see the brilliant full moon or the shower of falling stars or the rare comet? I have never regretted any of those *Now* decisions. But I have made decisions I regretted. And it wasn't until I learned to learn from my mistakes and to let the rest go, that I discovered an important concept. I didn't fail because I failed, but rather I succeeded because I tried.

As a mother of five children and now a grandmother of almost 12 grandchildren, you would think that multi tasking would be a major part of my life. And at one time it was. I could be listening on the phone to a friend's new woes of a broken heart, while playing chess with my kindergartener, and putting dishes away between my turns at the chessboard. But oh, what I was missing out on in the moment. It is a wonderful thing to be able to give your full attention to a friend, a child, or even a stranger when you are interacting with them. I know many books support and encourage multi tasking for greater efficiency, but they usually don't talk about the greater enjoyment of concentrating on the moment. For me, multitasking is often synonymous with diluting your experiences. I prefer the concentrated version of mindfulness in the *Now* moment, and the deeper levels of interaction that occur when you are focused at that moment.

When my children were young, I was amazed at their energy levels and I closely observed them to see where it all originated. I learned that when something isn't fun for a child, they usually choose not to do it. But if they are forced to do it, they will often get very creative and find a way to make it fun. *That* is what seemed to energize them whereas we as "mature adults" are drained when we do tasks that we dislike doing but we know we have to do them anyway. I too have learned to make many of those energy draining tasks fun. Mopping the floor? I rubber band sponges onto the bottom of my feet, turn on some 50's music and I dance as I mop my kitchen floor! Does that task drain me? No! It energizes me. But what about tasks like filing your IRS taxes? That's a fair question, and it used to be a drag for me. Now I simply enjoy learning where our money went and giving thanks that we made enough money to have to pay taxes. I like to remember when I drive on a new road, that I helped pay for that. And I like to go over my experiences for the year with my home business and cheer when I make a profit!

I think it was my grandmother that taught me "Without the stones, the brook has no song." When I have challenges or trials in my life, I wonder if they will be little stones creating small babblings in my "life brook" or whether they will be huge rocks that will create waterfalls. More importantly, one needs to recognize at what point does the sound of the babbling creek or the rushing waterfall cause stress and at what point does it bring joy and relaxation?

The sound of a waterfall is beautiful, so long as you are not in a canoe that is about to go over the waterfall's edge. The ability to allow trials and challenges to be in our lives, because they are an unavoidable part of life and yet not allow them to take us over the edge of the waterfall is vital to our ability to have joy in the *Now* moments every day. Oftentimes this ability is best developed through creativity. And don't you dare say you are not creative. Anytime you come up with a new thought or idea, even if a million other people have thought the same thing, as long as it is new to you, you are being creative. And the more you recognize that creativity, the more it will flourish and be reflected in your joy towards life.

Being able to creatively look at things from a different perspective often allows us to sit back and enjoy the song of the brook or the power of the waterfall, without being overcome by either. I remember the mother of a young softball player who got a small bug stuck in her inner ear and it was sending her into hysterics. Rather than taking her out of the game and going to the doctor or emergency room, the creative mother knew the trapped bug also had a problem. She simply put a towel over her daughter's head to create a dark space and then she held up a small flashlight by her daughter's ear. The bug soon flew towards the light and out of the young girl's ear. Creativity is often simply a matter of perspective. Perspective and a sixth sense.

Every morning when I wake up, I give thanks for my six senses. My sense of sight as I look out the window, my sense of hearing as I listen for the bird songs, my sense of smell as I give thanks nothing is on fire, my sense of touch as I reach over and feel my husband's arm and my sense of taste as I eat a fresh raspberry. That's five, so what is the important sixth sense I give thanks for every day? It is a combination of creativity and humor. It is this sixth sense that usually gives me a rope securely tied to a tree at the top of any waterfalls in my life. I can pull myself to the shore and have joy in the moment that I did not go over the edge. Someone once said, "Crisis plus time can oftentimes equal humor!" I used to turn a lot of calendar pages before I could laugh, now I extend the trust it will someday make me laugh so I go ahead and laugh now while I am still here.

I remember my 8 year old son's planned birthday party with a few of his friends, scheduled for right after school. Everything was ready and my Betty Crocker cake was baking but when the timer went off and I opened the oven door, I gasped to see that the entire middle of the cake had somehow sunk and fallen. I didn't have time to bake another cake or the budget to go buy one, so I called upon my sixth sense of humor and creativity. I filled the sunken part of the cake in with a black, dark chocolate icing, and then I set my son's plastic dinosaurs in and all around the "tar pit". Later I had several mothers call to ask for my recipe for the now famous Tar Pit Dinosaur cake.

Living in the *Now* has enhanced every part of my life. It is not only energizing and fun, but it creates true joy in life. And the more that you live your life in the *Now*, the more your future is impregnated with exciting possibilities that will someday give birth, while the negatives of your past lose their power to damper your joy now.

In one of the cup holders in my car, sits a bottle of bubble juice and a bubble wand. Whenever I am caught in a standstill traffic jam, especially on hot, humid summer days I open my moon roof and using the vent of my air conditioner, I let the cool air blow bubbles for me and the drivers all around me. Instantly I see frowns turning to smiles and drivers' giving me thumbs up as the bubbles escape out my moon roof. And then I see windows rolling down as people reach out to touch and pop the bubbles. It is such a simple thing, but it is an example of the best part of living in the *Now*. It is like getting a double scooped ice cream cone for the price of a single scoop when we can share the joy of *Now* with others.

The biggest secret I have discovered is the simplicity of living in the *Now*. It doesn't take more time, instead it creates *more* time. More time spent smiling and more time spent being true to yourself and your values and beliefs. My family knows my motto of SSABAT which stands for *Stay Strong And Bright And True*. I have learned that

I am best able to do exactly that when I live in the *Now*, knowing I am also attending to a brighter future and a less painful past. Yes, my Life's kite tail still has room for many more rag experiences to be added and as always, I think my kite may dip and swing at times, but mostly it will be flying high as I reach for the highest that is in me.

About the Author

57 years ago I was born Cathy Christine Berbert in Salt Lake City and then my family moved shortly afterwards to Ventura, California where I grew up. I raised a family of five children in our underground home and have been married to the love of my life, Larry Svacina since 1994. We are now blessed with 12 beautiful grandchildren. For years I was the lead tour guide for Harley-Davidson Factory in Kansas City, but since 1985, I am mostly known as The Marble Lady. (www.themarblelady.com) I have taught or helped teach thousands and thousands of children and adults how to play marbles and in 1992 was the first woman ever allowed to participate in the National American Adult Marble Tournament ---The Rolley Hole Tournament. My husband and I donated our famous marble collection to the Kansas City Toy and Miniature museum (www.toyandminiaturemuseum. org) where they built a large addition on to house the collection. I have a Kindness Marble Program and Shoot Marbles-Not Drugs program with youth and our Kindness marbles have spread around the world! My belief in God, my love of my family and friends and my appreciation for nature, and the joy I find in my varied community service all help me to fully appreciate the Now of every moment!

My Future is Defined by My Present
DeAnna Radaj

"There are 2 days in the week about which I never worry… 2 carefree days kept sacredly free from fear and apprehension. One of these days is yesterday. And the other day I do not worry about is tomorrow."
Robert Jones Burdette

In my personal journey of self-empowerment, confidence and becoming more comfortable in my own skin, *and* by default, becoming more successful in my business, was the ability to stay present and in the moment. While in my "previous life" of working in the harried world of retail management where everything is a "crisis", 1 store didn't get the right shipment of an advertised item, another is short staffed and a franchisee is having problems understanding their lease agreement, having a very detailed calendar with marketing, buying and hiring schedules that stretched 6 months into the future were how I lived my life. July you say? I was planning Christmas promotions and even buying for Valentine's Day. Forget about playing in the sun and enjoying grilling out by the pool…I had penguins to buy.

This was the course of my life throughout my 20's and into my 30's however, it was when I was 29 when my father died suddenly of a massive heart attack. He was 52. While my father died at a relatively young age, he was living his dream. He taught my brother and I the importance of getting out in nature (making us identify all the sounds… ugh), following your passions and life purpose, and not living your life for others. This was one of the most important lessons he left us. It was soon after the loss of my father, that more loss was to occur. In the next 4 years to follow I lost my 3 remaining grandparents, a close friend and my dog. It was also during this time that there was a group of friends who all lost their fathers the same time I lost my father (10 of us within a year).

It was in this "numb" phase, that my only goal was to get up in the morning, take care of what needed to be taken care of at work and my family, and then go right back to bed. There was no thinking about the future, but there was a lot of thinking about the past: what was never said, what was said, things that should have been done, the present was just something to get through. It was also during this time that I really vowed to never live a life of regrets or succumb to what I call the "coulda, woulda, shoulda" mindset that I try to teach/coach my clients now.

Having spent the better part of my life trying either to relive the past or experience the future before it arrives, I have come to believe that in between these two extremes is peace.
Author Unknown

For me, the hardest part of trying to live in the moment and be present was not living in the past. The future was to be planned and looked on with excitement at all that could and would be accomplished. After having lost so much in such a short amount of time, the past was easier to "deal with" as it was known, even if parts were sad. The present hurt to deal with for a long time. I reached a point in my mid-30's where it just became unbearable. I had a choice to make. I started doing some soul-searching on what it was exactly I wanted to do with my life. I rediscovered my love of writing, photography and teaching. I continued to learn about energy work, aromatherapy, Feng Shui and become more connected spiritually. I was feeling good again. I just needed to coordinate my work with my newfound (rediscovered) current life.

I quit my job and opened up my own retail stores to see if that was the key. It wasn't, but it was a start. I felt the creative juices flowing again, I felt inspired and more empowered. I ended up going back to school to work on my interior design degree. I did this while still running my company, but that finally gave. I sold or closed my stores to focus solely on my new path. I was a full-time student again (yikes).

While my full-time job stopped, my bills didn't. I still had a mortgage to pay, 2 new puppies to feed and gas to go in the car. I took a job as a hostess 3 times a week, a part-time marketing consulting job and this is the time I started developing my workshops. I used my teaching opportunities to start getting the word out about my new company, Bante Design, and establish my expertise and make some money at the same time. It was during this time, that my "being present" really started to get targeted. I had to be present in my life. With so much going on, I had to focus so I could make the most of all those moments: learning a new skill-set, teaching to a new audience new concepts and just being where I needed to be when I needed to be there.

After completing my interior design degree in a year, Bante Design was ready to take the world by storm. While the design services were what I thought the primary focus of Bante Design was to be, it ended up being the Education division of workshops that became the focus and where most of my success started to come from. The key to being successful in any type of teaching/coaching endeavor is to stay present… No matter how many times you give a workshop, it is always going to be the first time your audience hears it. You can't afford to go into cruise control. It must sound as fresh as it did, with content as current as possible; to keep your audience engaged.

It is from workshops and any type of live events that you are given a built-in audience to sell your products and services… It is imperative that you are engaged with them, listening to them and talking to them, not at them.

From a business standpoint, staying *present* has helped me establish great relationships with clients, audience members (workshops, radio, TV) and helping to inspire others. One of the best compliments I've ever received was from a workshop attendee at a Women4Hire career event. The workshop I gave was attended by over 200 people

– The Importance of Small Talk – and the comment was *"DeAnna made me feel like she was talking to me in my living room, not a hall with hundreds of people"*. It is through being present, responding to the audience (client's needs) and responding in kind, that helps to elicit responses like the one I got.

"Living in the moment" is also a key concept to one of my coaching programs and part of my design philosophy, Integrative Lifestyle Design. It is key, in my opinion, that you take control of your life, create the life you want (not what others want for you), and be proactive and not re-active to how you conduct your life. It is through de-cluttering (The Clutter Counseling program) where I "make" you go through all of your items and state if it's working for you or not, states who you are not who you were and if you even use it. Every item in your space must serve a positive purpose. You can't let the past, guilt, or the "coulda, woulda, shoulda" voices in your head (or from family or friends) get in the way of what you have in your space surrounding you.

Clutter is the "physical manifestation of your emotional baggage". If you don't LOVE it, USE it or NEED it, it must go. Period.

Through all of my design consultations, dealing with the clutter "issues" is key. Your "stuff" shows a snapshot of where you are, where you've been and what's holding you back. With too much stuff, the condition of your stuff & how well you maintain it, where you display/store it (Feng Shui) or even a lack of personal effects, says a lot. It is actually looking at your items, loving and using them and placing them properly throughout your space that can give you the feeling of support, empowerment and living in your space and enjoying it.

From a personal standpoint, looking at my journey to now, I have found that it is important to live in the moment as you don't know how many moments you have. From the early death of my father, to my grandparents, 3 of whom lived long lives, you don't know who you'll have, when or for how long. Make the most of those moments when you create them. That way, whether you are recalling activities and events when you're 90 and talking to your long-time best friend, or sharing stories as you eulogize a beloved family member, you'll have the comfort of knowing that you lived and experienced the "moment" and not just showed up while you worried about your carpool assignment the next Monday or an old grudge that you just can't let go.

> *"Yesterday is history. Tomorrow is a mystery. And today?*
> *Today is a gift. That's why we call it the present.*
> **Babatunde Olatunji**

About the Author

DeAnna Radaj, lifestyle design consultant/writer/radio show host is the owner of Bante Design LLC. They can enter a space and help to tweak (or remodel, re-design) the space to work better to suit its function and the lifestyle of the occupants of the space. Using Integrative Lifestyle Design, life quality can be increased and be supportive to any transitions occurring, lifestyle changes or health challenges. She is a nationally recognized speaker on healthy home design, color therapy/theory, psychology of clutter for adults and children, and a variety of business topics for the individual, small business owner and entrepreneur. For more information visit the Bante Design Web site at www.bantedesign.com.

A New World
Mary McManus

The present – the gift – living in the moment. Growing up in an alcoholic home after having contracted paralytic polio, I learned how to escape the present moment in my mind. I learned dissociation from my body to escape the pain of abuse. I developed obsessive compulsive traits and a Type A personality. On the outside looking in, one would say I was a success. I had an award winning career at the Department of Veterans Affairs, I was married to a man with a successful IT career, I lived in a house just outside of Boston and had twins who were honor roll students. Was I happy? No. Was I healthy? Definitely not. I could not live in the moment and feel a sense of peace, gratitude, joy, love or freedom.

Beginning in 1996, I experienced symptoms of post polio syndrome. The Universe/God was gently nudging me to awaken from my slumber. I ignored the gentle nudging and pushed myself beyond exhaustion. The more I ignored the symptoms, the more they tried to grab my attention. In July 2006 my symptoms went from a smoldering fire to a raging blaze. I experienced symptoms of weakness, fatigue, pain, tremors, shortness of breath, difficulty swallowing, numbness, tingling and the limp from my polio returned. By October of 2006, I no longer cared whether or not I woke up in the morning. All those years of self hatred, dissociation and having my thoughts travel to the past or to the future was a festering boil waiting to be lanced and cleansed with God's healing love. I prayed, but I prayed for God to release me from my worries. The answer to my prayer came in the gift of being diagnosed with post polio syndrome in December 2006.

I had no choice but to stop literally and figuratively running around. I was told by my team of doctors, physical therapists, occupational therapists and speech and language therapists that I had to make major lifestyle changes. I was told that I needed to quit my full time job. I went back into a leg brace and used a wheelchair at times for mobility. I used a cane and a wrist splint. I spent hours with my rehab team and began contemplating what my future would hold. Initially, fear gripped my soul and then, once I relaxed and surrendered and focused on living in the moment magic and miracles began to happen in my life.

I was blessed with healing angels who talked to me about caring for myself. They taught me how to be mindful. Because of the difficulty with swallowing, I had to learn techniques for mindful eating. I had to slow down and concentrate on taking small bites, using a dry swallow and chewing slowly. I could not talk while I ate. I learned techniques on connecting my mind to my body. During challenging rehab exercises, my mind could not wander. I had to focus on encouraging my nerves and muscles to connect to get stronger. Because of the breathing difficulties, I had to lie still and coax my diaphragm muscles to get stronger. Although my body shut down, I was beginning to feel the stirrings of a transformation. I was experiencing re connection to my Spirit and to God.

In February of 2007 as I contemplated my future, I sat very still. I felt the urge to create. Create what, I wondered? I went to my laptop and wrote the poem, "Running the Race". It was the first time I wrote about my experiences with polio. It's no surprise that it came out in rhyming couplets; my physical therapist, Miss Holy, when I was 5, would read Dr. Seuss to me before every painful physical therapy session to help me to relax. My Spirit was taking its first steps on the healing journey. In one of the couplets I wrote, "Celebrate my body creaks groans and need for a brace/While in my mind I focused on winning a 10K race." With that, poetry began to pour out of my soul. I felt as though I were taking dictation from God.

There is no better way to be living in the moment as when we create. I lose track of time when I write poetry and the powerful images that I created helped me to heal mind, body and spirit (along with leaving my full time job at the VA, intensive outpatient rehab, nutritional changes, implementing all of the suggestions of my rehab team, and initiating a practice of prayer and meditation). I felt as though I were taking dictation from God as I created two books of inspirational poetry. When I would be at the beach, I would sit and drink in the moment and write a poem about the experience. My soul awakened to a whole new world in which I paid attention to nature, to my body, to people and slowed down to experience and embrace each moment of my life.

Slowly my body began to come to life as my spirit flew free. I came out of the leg brace and hired a personal trainer to see if I could get a little stronger. That was in October of 2007. I still had difficulty getting off of a low toilet seat and was terribly deconditioned from the post polio syndrome and years of not paying attention to my body or to myself. My trainer was another healing angel. As we began to embark on a health and fitness journey, she would help me to intensely focus on the muscles and nerves I was coaxing back to life. I used writing poetry to intensify the experience. I practiced in between sessions and it all came down to being in the moment, living with intention.

In February of 2008, since I had reached my initial health and fitness goals, my trainer asked me what next? I said that I wanted to know what it's like to feel free in my body, to dance, to take a walk outside and then the words, "And I want to run the Boston Marathon for Spaulding Rehab as a charity runner" fell out of my mouth. She sent me off to trade in my polio shoes for running shoes and together, along with my husband and daughter, we embarked on the journey of a lifetime. The only way to train for a marathon is to be in the moment. I began by running for 30 seconds and walking for 4 ½ minutes. I could not think about the 26.2 mile course, I could only live in the moment and have the keen focus of training this body which had never run before to prepare to run a marathon – and not just any marathon, the Boston Marathon. I wrote poetic reflections on the Road to the Boston Marathon and blogged about my experience heightening my ability to live in the moment, to be still, to reflect and embrace the journey.

At 4:49 pm EST on April 20, 2009, my husband, daughter and I crossed the finish line of the Boston Marathon, 7 hours and 49 minutes after our early start with the other mobility impaired runners. It was a miracle run fueled by the love and prayers of so many. Everyone talks about living in the moment when you run the marathon; drink in every sight and sound and record it for your memory. I did just that focusing on the people in the crowd, the kindness of strangers, the screams along the route, the signs I saw which were messages from God letting me know that with God all things are possible. (That was written on one of the signs). Had I focused on getting to the finish line, there is so much I would have missed. That is a truism for life.

I begin every day with at least 45 minutes of meditation and prayer. I connect to my body and see what parts need healing and loving that day. On days that I do strength training, I have my water and focus on continuing to strengthen muscles and nerves to halt the progression of this 'progressive neurological disease.' I have a nutritious breakfast and eat mindfully. I read the Daily Word and a Daily Prayer Blog. I write in my gratitude journal. I check emails and see what's happening on Facebook. As my mind begins to wander or enter into the 'fear zone', I tame it and bring it back to the present. I take time outs during the day to meditate and write in my journal if I find that I am resorting to old habits. I get still and ask God how I can be of service today? What can I do for fun and relaxation? What do I need to do to fulfill commitments I have made for fund raising? I don't push for answers; I get still and let answers flow to me. I pay attention to signs. I take time for rest. I enjoy the journey and let the ebb and flow of life carry me to my various destinations. When I have interactions which stir up negative emotions, I pull out my spiritual toolbox to help me get centered again. I also like to pretend that I have amnesia and cannot remember any of the details. With post polio syndrome and something called, 'brain fog' that can actually happen. I reach out to others in love and to receive love. I spend a lot of time in nature, having a dialogue with God and experiencing God's love through others. I love my life now when once I can honestly say I did not care whether or not I woke up in the morning. I breathe deeply, get still, count my blessings and hear the Voice of God direct me to inspired action to fulfill my purpose in life; because I changed my world and now embrace the moment, I can be the change I want to see in the world. I donate 20% of book proceeds and fund raise for Hope Charitable Trust, a group of dedicated volunteers in India bringing the only medical and physiotherapy care to children and their families crippled by polio and cerebral palsy. I am so blessed with the healing I experienced in my life and the gift of learning how to live in the present, that I want to share that gift with the world. My hope is that I inspire you to not wait until the Universe hits you with a two by four to begin to live a life centered in the present moment. My hope is that my journey inspires you to re evaluate your life and see how you can slow down, simplify and appreciate the gift of the present.

"The Present"
Right now is the present and that's where I live
To precious life's moments, my attention I give.
'The past is over,' I say with a sigh
And cheerfully bid it a farewell goodbye.
The future's not here yet, so pull back the rein
And focus attention on the present again.

About the Author
Mary McManus is a Boston Marathon finisher who loves inspiring others with her healing journey of Polio and Post-Polio Syndrome. Her dream is to help create a Polio free world. She loves sharing her gift of gab and poetry as a writer and inspirational speaker. Mary started a new life and created a new world at the age of 53. For more information visit her website at www. NewWorldGreetings.com.

What's Your Attitude?
Gayle Nobel

I was sitting on the floor of the pediatric intensive care room with my husband. They had just wheeled the metal hospital crib, which contained our five month old son out of the room. His peaceful drugged slumber was a reprieve from the continuous seizures he had been having. He was being taken for tests.

A cat scan, a spinal tap. A baby his size should not need to have these tests. We should not even be here.

This was the beginning of a challenging life long journey. Our beautiful baby boy, Kyle, had been having seizures in our arms for the last few days. At first they were subtle and we weren't quite sure what they were. Gradually, they became more intense and therefore, obvious. He was stiffening, turning a deep blue (aka: not breathing), and rolling his eyes to the heavens.

I felt as if my world had just been pulled out from beneath me. How could this be? This was not supposed to happen to my son, to me. In the next few hours, we were to learn he had epilepsy. Despite the long list of great people with epilepsy rattled off by the neurologist, what I heard was that my son was now *damaged*. The future felt scary and so uncertain.

In the months to follow, we noticed our son was not developing typically for his age. It wasn't long before we discovered his developmental issues were severe. Epilepsy was only a small piece of the big picture. He had Autism, just like his uncle. Add to that, significant cognitive delays and motor issues which made up a package called "special needs".

This was not the motherhood dream I signed up for. I had planned to have a baby who would then grow up to be a "typical" child and do all the regular child activities. My baby would eventually develop into a wonderful young adult. Marriage and then some beautiful grandchildren were on my agenda. Though I had never articulated this vision, this was the life I expected.

What happens when you don't get the child you expect? What happens when you don't get the life you expect? What happens when things come your way which fall under the umbrella some would describe as "adversity"? Do you crumble or do you rise?

In the process of searching for programs and therapies to help my son, I stumbled upon a philosophy which changed my life. It's All About Attitude! It is my attitude that is going to determine my experience. It is my attitude which will affect the choices I go on to make and whether I decide to take the stance of a victim (poor me) or a victor (make the best of it).

I heard a man say he never wanted to look at his Autistic son and see terrible or tragedy. Most people, including me at that point in time, would have easily agreed that Autism was a tragedy. This was a pivotal moment. I knew I wanted to take a different path and attempt to embrace this beautiful attitude. I didn't know how I was going to do it because at first, I was miles from that way of thinking. However, I felt empowered when I became aware that my attitude was the key to a happy life and the only thing I had a chance of controlling.

My son Kyle is now a twenty-six year old man. He is severely impacted by his Autism and many other issues which comprise his special needs package. He requires extensive support in every area of his life and always will. He is an amazing person who has accomplished much given the obstacles he faces every moment of every day. Because of who he is, he has taught me to be a better human being in a myriad of ways.

I don't believe I would have this perspective if not for that pivotal moment twenty-three years ago when I made the decision to work toward living with a "glass half full attitude".

My son has a severe and lifelong condition. Living with, teaching, and taking care of him is my biggie, my greatest life challenge. I can't control Autism, but I can control my attitude about Autism. I choose to thrive versus merely survive.

What is *your* Autism, your challenge? Perhaps it is a health issue or an issue with a loved one. At one time or another, we all get to carry a heavy backpack. We all get some "Autism" plopped in our laps, the unexpected. Circumstances come our way that challenge us to rise to the occasion or crumble. Each day and each moment, we have a choice.

I have a lifelong practice of working on my attitude. I practice and I practice and I practice. And just when I may think I have it, I practice some more. Like repetitions when working an arm muscle at the gym, the attitude muscle grows and strengthens as I practice flexing it. There are many opportunities for flexing which show up every day in life.

What are the exercises that strengthen the attitude muscle? What are the practices that create "thrive"?

My attitude toolbox is overflowing with oxygen-rich tools for the care and maintenance of attitude. These tools help me live in the present moment, in the *Now*, rather than some imaginary world without a son with Autism. This box is packed with tools which remind me to slow down and treasure the moments.

Gratitude, breathing, yoga, writing, and anything that helps me live more in the present moment impacts my attitude one micro-movement at a time. It's all about the micro-movements, the baby steps which create small shifts in attitude and perspective. Like a growing flower, change happens slowly over time rather than in large chunks.

Where to start? Open the toolbox and you will find "Breathe". I titled my second book "Breathe" because it is so important. Stop "doing" for a moment. Take five deep breaths. Focus on breathing more slowly and deeply. Repeat as often as needed. Ahhhh. Breathing pops us into the *Now*, even if just for a moment. Breathing allows us to respond rather than react.

Peek in the toolbox again and you will see gratitude. Gratitude is the sweet nectar of life. Sip often. How? In "Breathe", I share the following: "At the end of the day, if it's been one of those days, making the decision to feel grateful makes gratitude real. I make a list of the things I love about Kyle (my son). I allow my hand to glide across the page as fast as it can. Even a list of just five things makes gratitude tangible and creates a tiny shift in my attitude. I'm always glad I did this because, once again, love wins, and it feels really good."

Take a closer look. There are many tools to make gratitude tangible. Grab a pen and paper. Start a gratitude journal. Or make a list of your accomplishments for the day. Or write a letter of appreciation to someone you may have taken for granted. And what was the best part of your day today? Ask yourself this question and even better, ask your spouse or your children just before they go to bed. This is where the good stuff lies. Gratitude impacts attitude which makes loving and living well real.

What else is lurking in the toolbox? You may find some yoga. Don't let the word "yoga" scare you if you are not familiar with it. You will not be told to twist yourself into a pretzel. At least not right away. Yoga is about awareness and mindfulness. Again, living in the *Now*. Yoga is about breathing. Breathing is the only part of the autonomic nervous system we can control. It slows the heart rate and affects body chemistry. Therefore, it is a way to change our physiology. Breathing is the express lane to experiencing a glimpse of the present moment.

These are a few of the tools I have accumulated over a lifetime of living with a son with Autism. They are my special elixirs, providing nourishment and fuel for living in the *Now* and for loving and living well.

I think back to our time in the intensive care unit with my baby Kyle. The life I expected to have ended that day. Instead, I began walking a different path filled with a different beauty. I learned to practice taking on life's challenges with grace as I live more in the *Now*. And guess what? Life is still good. Very good.

About the Author

Gayle Nobel is the coauthor of It's All About Attitude: Loving and Living

Well with Autism and the author of Breathe: 52 Oxygen-Rich Tools for Loving and Living Well with Autism. She holds a BA in Special Education, and directed an intensive home therapy program for 11 years for her autistic son Kyle, who is now 26. During that time she trained over 100 volunteer therapists and aides in the attitude she writes and speaks about. Originally from New York, Gayle is an author, inspirational speaker, parent mentor, and also a sister to a 50 year-old brother with Autism. She lives with her husband and three children in Arizona. In "Breathe", she offers support, inspiration, and hands-on tools in every chapter for living well with life's challenges. To learn more visit her website at www.AutismwithAttitude.com.

How are you?
Dagny McKinley

"How are you?" I ask my friend.

"I'm..."

"I need to pick up dog treats, washing to do, pictures to upload, great kiss last night, his lips, chapstick, toothpaste, finish two chapters of."

My friend's words never reached my ears. I had the nods and umm hmms down in place and when she made eye contact, I would break from my thoughts for a moment to squeeze in an appropriate comment, and then go back to the world in my head. The sad part was I couldn't even focus on one thought for long. Everything tumbled over one another. I was caught up in my insecurities and my entire world turned inward.

I was afraid to look out, to really take in the world around me, afraid of how I might be judged, or how I might be seen. And then I made a decision. I chose to go to Naropa University for my MFA in Creative Writing. Naropa University was founded by a Buddhist monk and one of the integral aspects of the program is being kind to both body and mind. So as I signed up for my eco-lit class and other fiction classes, I also signed up for meditation and body-mind centering classes.

Throughout my two-year program, I learned that the hardest person on the earth to love is me. I had always struggled with self-esteem issues and felt I wasn't good enough to be loved, to succeed, and to be alive. At Naropa, I learned to be kind to myself. In learning to love myself, I was able to open up to the world and look outward. I slowly came out of my busy head through meditation where the focus was always on the breath and thoughts that come and go were labeled 'thoughts' and allowed to float away while focusing on my breath. I learned to be in the moment - to appreciate that this moment will never come again. If I am living in the past or the future, then I am missing the *Now*. In essence I am missing out on my life.

I hike almost every day. When I used to hike, there was a period where I hardly noticed the world around me, until eventually after an hour, sometimes longer, I saw the trees and the sky and I heard the birds chirping. This was when I felt myself relax.

One of my instructors, Margot said something in class I will never forget. She said, "the colors out there, the bright yellow jacket, the smell of flowers, these are gifts for you. These are gifts that are given every day. Enjoy them." To this day, I take a moment out of every hike to 'see' the gifts that are given to me. When I see something beautiful, I think, *this is my gift*. When I stop to smell the wild roses, I know, this scent is for me to enjoy.

Since then, I have become more engaged in my world. I'm not going to lie and say I am 100% focused on the *Now* at every second, but my conversations, when I fully listen are much richer than when I'm trying to multi-task.

When I left Naropa, I left much of what I learned behind. I rarely meditate, although it calls to me. When I am in a place of deep struggle, I do meditate to clear my head. However, I took the notion of body and mind co-existing together very much to heart.

In order to balance out my work writing in front of a computer, I took a job at a dog sledding kennel as a tour guide. It was a way to force myself outside every day. On the coldest days, I would remember that everything, every type of weather is good and has its purpose. I have worked for three years with over 100 dogs. Every moment I am with them, I am fully present. When I walk through poop to pet each one of them, I look into their eyes, see how they are doing and accept their love as a gift to me.

I have also twice attempted the World Record for Most Hugs in 24 Hours. This was a big deal for me in several ways. First, I had to put myself out there and stand in front of strangers, saying I am good enough to be hugged. The first time, I felt like I was at a grade school dance, in the corner afraid no one would want to dance with me.

When I had my first hug, it was a relief. But I also had an opportunity to connect with thousands of people and for one second, I was able to share their energy and their love. Complete strangers gave love to me. I had to be in that moment to feel their needs, whether they wanted a tight hug, a light hug, a long hug, or a quick hug.

Today when I talk to people, be it strangers, or during a workshop I teach, or a talk I'm giving to kids, I listen, because I only have one second to listen to them and to answer them with full awareness. If my mind is somewhere else, it takes away from what I have to offer and from all they have to offer me.

I don't always take the time I need to listen to myself, to be as kind to myself as I could be, but I take a few moments every day to be in the present. Whether that's with my dog, or with my friends, I want to experience my life as its happening. I often think if this was the last time I would ever get to see a flower, how would I look at it, how would I try to remember it? If I knew this was the last conversation I was going to have with someone, would I wish I had really listened? Was there something they were trying to tell me that I could have helped them with? I have made mistakes not listening in the past, or only listening to what I wanted to believe, but now I listen at face value.

There is a world around me that is happening *Now*. It will happen with or without me. It's my choice whether or not I want to participate in it, or whether I will miss the sunshine falling on my face, or the aspen tree bending in the wind. It's my choice how the next conversation will go when I ask, "How are you?"

About the Author

Dagny McKinley received her MFA from Naropa University in Boulder, CO. She published her first book, in 2009 - 'Wild Hearts: Dog Sledding the Rockies' - www.DogSleddingTheRockies.com about her experiences working as a dog sled guide in Steamboat Springs, CO. She contributes to various magazines and on-line journals, as well as publishing the on-going fiction series 'Audrey Rose,' www.SweetAudreyRose.com.

Living in the Here and Now
Jill Nussinow

Finding a way to live fully every day has taken time. When my son Shane, now 17, was born, I seemed to have lost my focus on being mindful. I was so busy making sure that my baby was cared for, and that I got dressed each day, I forgot what it was like to have my own life. I say that it took almost 4 years to find myself again but when I did, my life was forever changed.

I began taking yoga classes once a week the year that Shane would turn four. For some reason, after attending my first class, which offered on a Friday night, my husband suggested that I return the next week. Generally, my husband wouldn't have wanted to be home alone with Shane after a hard week's work but Rick must have seen something shift in me, which I couldn't see myself. I think that it was the first time since Shane's birth that I really made time for myself, and had an opportunity to connect my mind with body and spirit.

I continued to attend yoga at least once a week for a while, until I started going twice a week or more. What I began doing was taking the time to be mindful each day. I continue doing this to this day. Being mindful has served me well. I realize that I am not in control of anything except my own actions. I've vowed to find something each day for which to be grateful. I often do this first thing in the morning and then I can move on.

No matter what the event and how it seems to be, being present is a gift. When my father passed away in 2009, it was obviously not a good time. I had a chance to visit with him a couple of times before he was gone, and although I was upset while sitting there with him I was fully present, speaking to, and with him as if life mattered, which it did and still does.

I often say that I am "rushing slowly". There are few things in life where being a few minutes late really matters. Paying attention and being mindful has rewards that aren't tangible and helps me spin my view so that the colors seem brighter, the tastes more robust, the aromas more enticing and the textures more full.

However you get to your mindfulness practice, through yoga, meditation, stopping to take a breath daily makes a huge difference in your body, mind and spirit. No matter what is going on around me, I've found a way to stand strong and enjoy the moment, for that's all we really have.

About the Author

Jill Nussinow, aka The Veggie Queen™, is a culinary educator, Registered Dietitian and cookbook author of The Veggie Queen™. Vegetables Get the Royal Treatment who teaches people about food and nourishment. She often spends class time getting her students to take a deep breath and express gratitude for what's on the plate before them. Her website is www.theveggiequeen.com

Back to Innocence
Paul Challenger

Living in the world of the here and now, without the pulling and tugging of the past, and fears of the future does not often appear feasible to us humans. But, it is possible to those who seek to challenge the norm. Looking through the eyes of a mind that is still, calmness floods the entire being which in turn creates room to make conscious decisions fruitfully.

As a Hypnotherapist, my aim is to create conscious change within the subconscious minds of my clients. This doesn't mean that the subconscious is more important, but the fact that the conscious mind is constantly interrupted because of the storage of the subconscious mind, a part of the human psyche that is much deeper and larger than the conscious mind we use daily. We must deal with the subconscious in order to truly be in the here and now. Being in the here and now requires optimism in the way we perceive our lives on a daily basis. The way we approach situations that may not go the way we entirely hoped it to be, or an inside reality that just hasn't really fit the world we expected to be in.

As children look upon the world they take everything in without analysis and judgment. They immerse all their senses in the world around them. The peace that fills them is the conscious life humans could enjoy eternally by living the here and now lifestyle. Somehow, this peace the child so seemingly enjoys makes a turn for the worst as we age. Where did the peace go? Life's stressors seemed to find their way to the top of our minds; nothing seems to match the child's internal make-up of peace and trust. We can enjoy the here and now if we simply allow ourselves to let go.

It brings joy to see and hear children playing doesn't it? Just looking at them we notice their present centered living. No worries of the world to stress about, no thinking to put their minds into overdrive, they are simply made up of sweet innocence that is playful. This type of living allows them to take in vast amounts of information. The slow here and now that we see in children gives them the ability to become slow to anger, slow to fear, slow to worry, etc. Why can't we return to the conscious living we enjoyed as children? We can and when we do we will enjoy the endless possibilities of the present. See you in the *Now*.

About the Author

Paul Challenger is a certified Clinical hypnotherapist at the Da Vinci Centre in Grand Cayman. A native of the Cayman Islands, Paul has studied with many different well known and respected hypnosis instructors. His venture into the field of hypnosis and hypnotherapy has taught him that we are responsible for our own actions and what we do with our thoughts.

Satori Green
Donna W. Hill

All is illusion: let it go, and all is in order: let it come; in India, enlightenment (Samadhi) with the eyes closed; in Japan, enlightenment (Satori) with the eyes opened.
Joseph Campbell

Sometimes, a word -- especially an uncommon one -- grabs our imagination and holds on for dear life. Embracing it, we find an ethereal talisman, a guardian of the heart. When I first read the above quote, I was stopped in my tracks. All is in order; let it come ... *Satori*... with the eyes open. This was not the first time I had come face to face with the idea of embracing the present. I was already captivated by Verdandi, the Norse goddess of the present. Satori seemed to go hand in hand.

In the '80s while pursuing my music career in Philadelphia, I studied the Alexander Technique – a method of movement re education – and Tai Chi. Both disciplines emphasized cultivating an awareness of the present. Centering myself in the moment and being aware of my surroundings would help me respond to whatever came along.

But, my fascination with the present was not merely a quest for physical grace and poise. It was the answer to the most profound challenges of my life. Born legally blind from the degenerative eye disease Retinitis Pigmentosa, I floundered for decades in that misty world between normal vision and blindness. Too sighted to receive Braille and other non-visual skills, I was too blind to succeed without them. The philosophy was: if you could still "see" to read print, you should read print. It was irrelevant that doing so took obscenely inordinate amounts of time, resulted in ongoing headaches, meant you had little time for anything vaguely resembling a normal childhood and that you were doomed to fall behind academically and socially despite your efforts.

After five years of piano lessons, during which I learned to memorize music so I wouldn't have to look at it, I found my vision slipping beyond the point of being able to learn the more complicated pieces my hands could then play. When I quit, it broke my mother's heart, but no one had any alternatives. The frustration of trying to keep up and falling further and further behind was accompanied by the pain of constant bullying. As it became clear that no help was coming, I developed a seething resentment and rage.

Surviving in the face of these realities was a matter of keeping this rage in check. Thoughts unlinked to the here and now were of two kinds – fretting over the past and worrying about the future. Neither was tolerable. I found solace in nature when I filled my mind with awareness of the present. With no nagging unfinished business and no dire predictions of what was to come, I could find peace and the possibility of re-writing the scripts which had been emblazoned in my psyche.

This has enabled me to achieve some success. Graduating from college, living independently, pursuing my life's work and finding love – all things that people assured me were impossible (often in the most humiliating and public of ways) – have all happened.

I taught myself to play guitar and began writing music in high school. Not until I graduated from college did I receive my first guide dog and taught myself Braille. While in Philadelphia, I recorded three albums of my songs. My coverage, as a volunteer, of the Carter inauguration marked the first time national press credentials were awarded to a blind reporter from a radio reading service for the blind.

I built a career around my music; first as a street performer and later as a presenter at school assemblies and other music-based programs. I encouraged others to pursue their dreams and refuse to allow their circumstances to dictate the outcomes of their lives.

Were there set-backs? Many. It has always been easy for me to fall into doubt and despair. I am not one of those people for whom the light of self-assurance burns with an unerring consistency. I don't have a sense that all will work out well, that I am destined to achieve my goals. Despite the crushing defeats, however, I remain aware of one simple reality: I don't want the sad predictions to be true.

In the midst of my successes, my world was threatened. At 40, I found a lump in my breast. At first, having breast cancer wasn't the problem. I was working on my third album. We were going to use it to market my songwriting skills. After surgery and radiation, I returned to the studio and finished the project. The week after sending the master and cover art to be transformed into CDs, however, I found a lump in the other breast. After treatment, I didn't have the funds or energy to run around Nashville. My dreams were blowing up in my face and I didn't know how to proceed.

It took years and a move to the Endless Mountains of Pennsylvania to refocus my thinking. I stopped writing music, thinking it would give me space to envision new possibilities. That only lasted until 9/11. I also started working on a fantasy novel. That required learning to use a computer with text-to-speech software.

The computer allowed me to submit an electronic version of one of my songs to the volunteer-run nonprofit Performing Arts Division (PAD) of the National Federation of the Blind (NFB). I was asked to donate "The Edge of the Line" to PAD's "Sound in Sight" project, a multi-genre compilation of original tracks and covers by blind recording artists, which funds projects including a scholarship.

I was horrified to realize that things had actually gotten worse for blind kids since I was in school. In those days, 50% of America's blind kids learned Braille. Now, it's 10%. Unemployment is 70% for blind adults. Nonetheless, blind people are successful as lawyers, mechanics, journalists, chemists, engineers and in many other fields. The difference is Braille. Of the blind people who work, over 80% read Braille. Despite the availability of audio books and talking computers (both wonderful, irreplaceable tools), Braille is the only tool which can give true literacy to blind people on a par with print.

The shock of realizing that little kids are still suffering as I did spurred me into action. I soon learned that the skills I had developed while promoting my music were transferable. Now, as a volunteer PR person for both PAD and the NFB of PA, I attempt to get the story out about what blind people can do and the obstacles we face. I also write for the online magazines American Chronicle and Suite 101. I cover not only blindness issues but other topics such as wildlife conservation, health, music and knitting.

My novel is essentially done. Satori Green in the Verdandi Valley is a place of spiritual/magical awakening for my two heroes -- a couple of 14-year-old refugees, including a girl, who, like me, is a songwriter dealing with vision loss, prejudice and an irrepressible notion that physical sight should be unnecessary for social equality.

About the Author

Donna W. Hill is an author, singer/songwriter, recording artist, speaker and avid knitter in rural Pennsylvania. A 19-year breast cancer survivor, she writes on topics ranging from blindness and special education to wildlife conservation, health, knitting and folk music for several publications. Donna will soon publish her first fantasy novel The Heart of Applebutter Hill.

My Artist's Way
Cyndi Ingle

Artists aren't an "elite" breed; we ALL have the capacity to grow spiritually through creative pursuits.

Remember the INXS song from the late 80's, The Devil Inside? Well I have a new take on the theme of that title: we all have an *artist inside* — and lately, I've discovered mine.

It all started when I got a new memory card for the sweet little Olympus digital camera I've been using for the past six years. Suddenly instead of being able to take 30 measly photos at a time, I could fire off a mind-blowing 3,500!

Not only did it give a new meaning to the phrase from American Beauty, *Kodak Moment*, it's opened up a whole new universe of artistic freedom and ultimately, self-realization, to me.

This purchase meshed perfectly with a recent resolution to get out of my office for an actual lunch break at least three times a week. With a renewed interest in self-expression, I decided to explore the gritty city I work in, snapping images as I strolled.

Walking around the downtown core of a metropolis which is transitioning from a manufacturing economy to one focused on education, healthcare, and arts and culture provides for many surreal juxtapositions.

Point-and-click skyward: century-old architectural flourishes on buildings. Ground-level: hidden treasure (or not-so-hidden trash).

A brief litany of what I've discovered, courtesy of my fellow citizens:

- A pile of randomly arranged socks
- DVD porn, lost in a snow drift
- A veritable panorama of "Beware of dog!" and one "Beware of Wife" signs

Who knew that I'd also find a bong carved from an apple, or a culvert covered in obscene graffiti near my relatively upscale home?

My work-day photography journeys are really a form of meditation (although since I'm strolling around a city with über crack and poverty issues, my mind watches my back. What I enjoy is the solitude of exploring at a natural pace. I'm present, and living for this moment, not dwelling on the past or thinking about the future.

Sometimes the scenes I shoot boost that sense of Being-ness. Recently, I visited a 200-year-old cemetery, which radiated an ethereal beauty and presence. This photo session sparked even more creativity. Afterwards I used some of my cemetery photos, old jewelry, tarot cards, fabric and a metal box to create a shrine-like installation called "*Say Yes to Everything*."

As I crafted, "Say Yes," I realized that self-discovery creeps up when you least expect it.

A little self-truth: while I'm taking photos as a medium of self-expression, I'm also doing it to stroke my ego. After returning from a photography pilgrimage my ritual is to rush to download the photos to my computer, post on Facebook, and email links to my friends and acquaintances. I bask in the positive comments that flow back.

But taking it a step deeper into manifesting a deeply-personal art has allowed me to rediscover an intimacy with my own curiosity and creative gene (a spark we all share). It doesn't matter if we have formally studied art, are making money from it, or are defined by others as an "artist." I believe an artist is inside of every living being.

Aboriginal people world-wide recognize this hard-wiring in humans much more than we in the industrialized world. Each member of the tribe participates in singing, dancing and playing simple instruments.

Let's embrace our birthright to express ourselves in the artistic form of our choice. As well as immediately making you more present, welcoming art into your life can be a healing experience that will propel you along a path to self-discovery. I've started to amble down that path, and it all began with a simple memory card!

Lately, I've been becoming more interested in taking photos of people, and I'm planning my first photography show! It's all a continuum of artistic expression that continues to grow.

About the Author:

Cyndi Ingle graduated with a degree in Anthropology from the University of Toronto and studied Journalism at Sheridan College. After leaving Sheridan College Cyndi launched a freelance writing career that populated a variety of publications. Some of her favorite celebrity interviews are Phyllis Diller, the Ramones, Garth Brooks, and talking to Jane Arden about bras. Cyndi currently works as the community manager for a spirituality website called www.SoulsCode.com.

On Top of the Mountain
Alex Allred

My father and I both have a weird fascination with the obituaries. In fairness, my father wrote obituaries just out of college in the late 1950s for the Dallas Morning News. Even after he began a career in the military, his interest in the obits remains and, apparently, was passed along to me.

As I read them, I always ponder two things: Who are these people and if they had a choice, what more would they want their own obituary to say. It's a bit morbid but I cannot help but wonder and over the years, I've begun to weave my own obituary.

I want it to say it all. I want my own obituary to be a drama, a comedy, a romance and an adventure!

I want it to read that Alexandra Powe Allred was an author, a magazine editor, the first U.S. National champion for the women's bobsled team and named Athlete of the Year by the United States Olympic Committee. I want it known that when women were told they could never slide competitively, Alex was one of the first women to travel overseas to compete in the World Cup, that she made friends with bobsledders around the world and even tried her hand (and body) at skeleton.

I want my family and friends to cheer – not cry, as they listen to how I donned an attack-dog training suit, test drove the Volvo Gravity Car in Orange County, California only to have the brakes fail as I headed toward an intersection at the bottom of a mountain and stepped in beefalo poop (a cross breed between cows and buffalo) while sprinting across a field all in the name of a good story.

Of all the reckless and harebrained ideas I had, perhaps playing women's professional football as a defensive end, when clearly I had no idea what I was doing, tops my list. Sports Illustrated wanted the "inside scoop" of playing in the WPFL and at the age of 36 and mother of three, I was "it." But after countless bone crushing plays, a broken hand and dislocated arm, Sports Illustrated returned the favor by killing the story. It never went to print and, honestly, I'm okay with that. Even with my disfigured pinky, I would never change a thing.

I earned my second black belt while pregnant with my third child and at the age of 45, am currently training for my second marathon. It is grueling and challenging and difficult. Over the years, I've been injured so many times; I cannot list all the injuries. Not so long ago, I went to a chiropractor. As I filled out the information sheet, I paused over the three lines provided under the heading, "List medical conditions and/or injuries." I simply wrote, "See me." The list is too long to write or I might face a new injury – hand cramp.

My mother can only shake her head at me. Where did you come from? But I cannot imagine living my life on the sidelines. I cannot imagine not knowing the thrill of racing down a mountain, running from a beefalo or hearing that horrific, spine-tingling *ka-blink* sound as the brakes give on the Gravity Car.

It is, to say the least, a thrill!

People always ask me *how* I do what I do, from where do I draw the courage or even find the time. My answer is this: Be fearless but be kind. These are the words of a living-in-the-moment warrior.

I remember when I was playing professional football, a coach continued to give me one simple instruction: Don't let the shadow fall on your left shoulder.

What?!?!

What was that supposed to mean?

Before each play, each time having just dusted off the dirt and grass off my body, I would ask another veteran what that meant. But they would only smile and shake their heads. They wouldn't tell me as I would have to figure it out myself. Eventually, after too many hits to count, I learned that it meant I shouldn't allow the offensive player (the oversized, drooling Amazon on the opposite of the field) get on the outside of me, thus allowing her to come around and sack my quarterback. In the short term, the lesson for me was that I truly had no idea what I was doing. Long term? It was one of the most exhilarating times of my life.

Be fearless but be kind.

All too often, people miss out on an opportunity because they are afraid to try something new or challenging and worse, looking like a fool. But I assure you, when you are pumping your fists, face turned up toward the sky, trying your hardest to outrun an enraged beefalo so that you can, at the last minute, fling yourself over a fence, you make long lasting friends. These seemingly reckless actions leave previously stony-faced cowboys to laugh so hard they cannot form a complete sentence for almost two minutes after the beefalo sprint. When you step outside your box and into a bull pen, you make friends.

As for time, I would always assure people, there is plenty of it! To this sentiment, I had always meant that if people would push away from the television set and the computer, they could find time to engage more in life's adventures. But when I met Marshall Allen, I had a better appreciation for that statement.

Marshall Allen is a Captain with the Fort Worth Fire Department who became a quadriplegic following a freak bicycle accident. As our friendship developed, he redefined how I viewed life and, specifically, my "be fearless but be kind" motto. He said, "I think that there was a reason this happened to me. If people can see someone as large and healthy as me stricken by a truly bizarre incident, then maybe it will make them take a second to look at their own mortality and the fragile nature of their existence. If it takes them seeing me in a wheelchair to do that, then that's fine with me. You need to tell your wife or husband everyday that you love them. Tell them how important they are to you. Tell your children you love them and give them your time. Do the things that you want to do today. Tomorrow is not promised to anyone."

Together, Marshall and I wrote the book, *Swingman*, a story about faith, friendship and his fateful bike ride. But our journey, his zest for life and unconquerable spirit also made me reevaluate my living-in-the-moment philosophy. It's not about rocketing down an icy mountain or outrunning livestock. It is about the very thing that Marshall said. Tomorrow is not promised to anyone.

Not long ago, I worried over an obituary. It featured a young person with a smiling picture, date of birth, time of death and a list of survivors. That was all. And I wondered how had this young person lived and died? So few in years, was it a good life? And, again, I thought of my own obituary and how I want it to read. I want it to say that in my life I raged and roared, I laughed and loved, I made friends and kept them, I honored family and always tried to protect God's green earth. I accepted challenges, though often scary, just to see if I could and was not afraid to be the fool. I was fearless. I was kind. And that I could, by damn, out run a beefalo!

About the Author

Alexandra Powe Allred won the U.S. Nationals in September 1994, making sports history as she was named to the first women's bobsled team. When the United States Olympic Committee named her Athlete of the Year, it was the beginning of a lucrative sports career as a bobsledder, martial artist, and professional football player. Alexandra is now an adventure writer for a number of national publications, the editor of a community magazine and author of Swingman: What a Difference a Decade Makes. *She continues to work as a fitness instructor in Midlothian, Texas, where she lives with her husband and children. She most recently blogged for NBC during the Vancouver Olympics in "all things bobsledding" and continues to save turtles from the side of the road whenever possible! To learn more about this amazing woman visit www.AllredBooks.com.*

It Is What It Is
Kristina Anderson

My oncologist says that people who have had cancer have found their inner soul. This is certainly true for me.

To survive the emotional upheaval and fear that accompanies cancer – especially after treatment is over – I have had to find a way to live my life *along side* cancer, and I've done it through the practice of mindfulness. While cancer introduced me to my inner soul, mindfulness has taught me how to love it and understand it, and it has brought me to a place of peace I never thought I would reach.

Before cancer I danced around the edges of mindfulness. I dabbled, I didn't. I played with it, and then walked away. I dipped my toes in it, but was too steeped in my way of life to allow it to make a difference.

I'm 62. In my late 30s, life began to seriously spiral out of control. I was a single mom managing a large independent bookstore, and my stress level was causing sleepless nights and chaotic days. Yet working in a bookstore meant I had a library about mindfulness at my fingertips. I read books on eastern philosophy, Zen Buddhism, soulfulness, and mindfulness. Most of what I read struck one cord or another but as I look back on those days, what I was missing from my search was practice. And it took me a long time to realize it.

Early in my cancer treatment, I learned about breath. My breast cancer surgeon showed me a short exercise on deep breathing that helps heal the wounds in the chest of a woman who has gone through breast surgery. I began to practice taking deep, slow breaths to fill my chest with oxygen. I would close my eyes and envision healing, love, and peace entering my body with each inhale. I did this, and in doing so, I began to bring the practice of mindfulness into my every day.

When I finished what I call my big guns treatment (chemotherapy and other intravenous drugs), I felt at a loss. As many cancer patients do when treatment is over, I asked what's next. The doctors tell you to go back to work, go back to your life as it was before cancer (no thanks). But for me and many patients, what comes next isn't about going back. You move forward and forge a new normal. You could go about your days just as you did before the big C but do you really want to? And most people can't. Cancer changes everything. It changes you, your family, and everyone and everything close to you. On top of that, it opens the door wide to the possibility of recurrence and poses the question, "what if it comes back?"

And that's where I got stuck, and that's where practicing mindfulness saved me. I started attending a yoga class for cancer patients. I loved it from day one. Although I had practiced yoga and meditation in the 1970's, my practice at that time lacked commitment and understanding. This time was different. I became conscious of how mindfulness changes us, and being mindful starts with noticing our breath.

Today, I put mindfulness first above all else. If I let it, it can get buried under deadlines and to-do lists, and sometimes I have to put Post-it Notes above the kitchen sink, on the bathroom mirror and on my computer screen as a reminder to breathe. To be mindful. To practice being quiet and present. It's easy to forget to breathe. Sounds strange, I know, but think about it. Breathing is automatic, unless you're affected by pulmonary conditions. It happens whether you think about it or not. But when stressed, I have a tendency to hold my breath, and I am usually unaware that I'm doing it.

Through yoga, I have learned how to breathe consciously and with purpose. Something as simple as breathing can be easily overlooked, yet when we are conscious of our breath, we are living in the present. It sounds so simple, but for me, as for many people, it wasn't.

Today my number one priority is my health. I eat an anti-cancer diet, I exercise, and I practice being mindful – of my life, my breathing, my health, my days, my nights, and those I love and those who love me. When I allow stress – and I say allow because I do have control over it – I stop whatever I'm doing and breathe deeply. I may also begin playing with slowness—a practice that is directly connected to being mindful. I move in slow motion. I rise from my chair and begin walking in slow motion. This practice serves to remind me that where my attention goes, my power goes.

Here's what mindfulness has taught me:

I can breathe into physical pain and get instant relief from it.
I can let go of that which I can't control.
I can love easier.
I can live without the fear of death.
I can be more patient.
I can live today and not worry about tomorrow.
I can be present to those around me, including strangers.
I must be present to be mindful of life's mysteries.
That it's okay to be silent, and through silence I find peace.

Mindfulness has reminded me that everything is made of energy – the chair in which I sit, the bed in which I sleep, the table where I eat my food, the paper on which I write, the clothes that protect my body. And all of it and I are connected. Mindfulness has taught me that for *Now*, in this moment, I can be free.

About the Author

Kristina E. Anderson is President of EasyRead Writing, LLC, a plain language and health literacy firm established in 2002. As a specialist in plain language and health literacy, she brings an understanding of language, literacy and audience to for-profit and non-profit communications in the health and science fields. She writes for culturally diverse, low literacy and general audiences and has experience preparing materials for translation into other languages as well as conducting focus groups and readability testing and analysis. Kristina has a B.A. in cultural anthropology from the

University of New Mexico and is a member of the National Science Writers Association.

The Beauty of the Moment
Denise Krochta

Have you ever stopped to think that tomorrow might not come? What if you knew that today would be your last day? Do you ever go from here to there and when you get there realize that, in your mind, you were planning something that would be happening at a later date, time, and place? Do you ever go to the movies and realize that you missed a very relevant part of the movie because your mind was somewhere else?

Let's go back to the second question. Think about it. If you had 24 hours left and knew it, how would you spend them? Three of my siblings have died at young ages. The oldest was 40 years old. Two of the three were younger than I was. This often brought these thoughts to mind. I think it is human nature to think about this after young people die. But, we usually only think about it for a short while and then dismiss it and continue our usual mode of existence. For me and for many that includes lots of time spent physically in one place and mentally in another.

It was not until years after the deaths I mention above, that crisis, sadness, anxiety and frustration returned to my life. Worry, worry, worry. Projecting. The "what ifs" of the past and the "what ifs" of the future almost completely occupied my mind. This time my reaction was radical. I began to think, again, about making my time count, making it mean something. I began my journey into a life of learning to live in the present moment.

I am a practical person. I am a patient person. Changing from a distracted and preoccupied person to someone who can focus on the moment, I knew, would not be easy nor would it be immediate. I was willing to give it a valiant effort. I expected it could save my life. And, in many ways, it did.

In the beginning, each day I would catch myself projecting and worrying about the past or the future, at least 100 times. Each time I would catch myself and direct my thoughts to what was happening in my life at that particular moment. I would focus on the details and try to experience *Now*. This took a lot of hard work and concentration. Sometimes by the end of the day I had to take a break, because in those early days, I was exhausted. But, perseverance paid off. Big time!

After years of putting minute by minute together to experience each on its own, I will never regret the hard work. Today, distraction does come. There is minimal time worrying, even in the midst of drama and chaos, and my life is calm and serene when it should be and exciting and enlightening when it can be.

At this time in my life there is no wasted time. Waiting in lines, wherever, now that I am *aware* I have lots of entertainment. Sometimes I'm so busy watching what is going on around me that I hope the wait can be just a little bit longer. There is so much to see, hear, feel, and ponder.

Previously, I could be anywhere and much happened around me that I would never experience. Today, I realize that I spent much of my life not seeing because I was not looking with my mind, only with my eyes.

Each morning I wake up and let the dog out. There is so much to experience at that very moment. I look and *Now* I see. The flowers in my garden are partially opened and the bees and the butterflies (which had always been illusive in the past) can be seen busily beginning their day. The dew is dripping off the roof and the clouds in the sky form unique patterns and colors as the rising sun shines from behind them. The neighborhood hawk is looking down at us from the palm tree in the center of the driveway, as he does each morning. Speaking of the dog, the moment she walks out the door she stops to scan the yard for something to chase. She is completely focused on her environment. I've learned a lot of this from my dogs, actually. You see, dogs live in the moment, for the moment, and seem to be very focused on the goings on of that moment. I don't think they think much about the future.

As my day progresses, even what many would consider the mundane daily activities will bring a smile to my face at the strangest times. While sitting at a red light I often am attracted by something small that would never have gotten my attention in the past. I've been especially amused by spiders on my windshield, often continuing to watch what will happen to them when my car begins to pick up speed after the stop. Or I'll notice the expression on the face of a baby in a stroller as the mom walks in the cross walk at the light. Babies always make me smile.

It is my experience *Now* that I can enjoy myself no matter what I am doing and where I am. My husband likes to go to the home improvement store, and he likes me to accompany him. For many years, this was such a boring and unnerving chore for me, but I did it for my husband. When I began my transition to focus and experiencing each moment, even this experience changed. Instead of just wishing it to be over I began to pay attention to what was around me. I was amazed by the different kinds of people seriously enjoying their home improvement experience. I noticed the customer service people, some who were having good days, and some who were obviously having not so good days. I began to actually look at some of the items in the store and learn about things that I couldn't even identify at first. I realized that my original bad attitude really a waste of good time. There was a lot to learn here.

Every couple of months I go to get my hair cut. A simple activity you might think. Each time I do this someone washes my hair. During that time I've learned to pay strict attention to the feel of the warm, then cool water, the smell of the shampoo and conditioners, and especially the touch of the person shampooing my hair. It's like getting a massage as a bonus for the price of a haircut.

These are the many simple ways to practice living in the moment. When we have special plans like vacations, family celebrations, alone times in a beautiful and quiet place, we can really hone our skills and make these events even more special than ever. We begin to see *awe* in many (what we might have originally considered boring or common) things. We begin to recognize the small *miracles* around us every day. We notice that our bodies are less tense and there seems to be less stress in our lives.

As I said before, this is a simple concept but not easy. The rewards are never ending. Think about this. At the particular moment we are pondering the things of our choice we cannot worry and stress about the chaos and drama in our lives. Each moment we choose to focus on the very moment we are experiencing, chances are there is nothing to worry about or cause us stress. It is important that we take moment by moment. If we put these moments together it is easy to come up with some stress free and worry free time before you know it.

As I said, I am a practical person. I am not unrealistic and I am not idealistic. Many would consider this "living in the moment" thought process something out of the ordinary and not for the general population. This is not the case. For those, like me, who need to regain a sense of calm and sanity in a life surrounded by drama and chaos, "capturing" the present moment as often as possible can make this happen.

Anyone can do this. Try it. You'll like it!

(*For clarification of purpose: This is part of a plan that worked for me during some extremely stressful years of my teenage son's addiction to drugs.*)

About the Author

Denise Krochta grew up during the 50's and 60's on the East coast of the US. She has a BA degree from Indiana University, Bloomington, in foreign languages. After college, her career in International Business took her to places around the globe. Traveling, meeting and learning about people and their values and traditions, have since been an integral part of her life. Denise is married and has two grown sons. She and her husband live in Florida with their energetic boxer pup. Denise is the author of "Sweat: A Practical Plan for Keeping Your Heart Intact While Loving an Addict." For more information visit her website at www.DeniseKrochta.com

Act of Fulfilling = Being in the Moment = Happiness
Kita Szpak

If you look up the word "fulfill" in the dictionary, you will find it means to "accomplish", "carry out", "achieve", and "bring to pass". These words don't quite fire up the imagination as much as "realize", "satisfy", "make good", and "perfect" – words that not only embody the completion of a task but the emotional state of the person who is completing the task. When you fulfill and are fulfilled by "accomplishing" your goals and "realizing" your dreams, perfect balance is manifested from within and without effortlessly. This is what we call *happiness*.

Let's explain this further by picking up on the idea back to the time you were young and could do something really well effortlessly. You liked doing it because you were good at it. The hours flew by as you "lost yourself" in your activity. Time stopped and you were in the moment so keenly that you became what you were doing – what you were creating. It felt great and you were very happy.

Think of a recent situation when you've been happy. Was it at work when you were completing the web redesign? Was it when you were laying the final stones for your patio? Was it when you were scraping off the old paint from an antique chair you just bought? Was it when you started writing your book? When such moments are replicated and you move from one to the next easily, you are in the flow. You are fulfilling and being fulfilled in the same instance. Being in the flow is the Universe's way of telling you that you are where you are supposed to be – when this happens, you are happy. And if there is an ever-constant fluidity in your life, chances are you are not only happy but also *fulfilling your life purpose*.

In the past, I've often thought that being happy meant living out an almost-heroic existence where I am saving the world from certain calamity or dramatically stating my views in an international forum of great thinkers who are hanging on to my every word. I smile now as I read what I've just written. Wisdom and life experience tell me that it is precisely in the small gestures, that accumulate into bigger actions where I find the essence of "being in the moment", and of being happy. And if I repeat these instances of fulfillment effortlessly, then I am also following my life purpose.

I was out on my after-work run along the river a while back, and jogged into my favorite stretch of trees – pine trees to be exact. As I ran alongside of them, I spontaneously reached out to touch their green needles. It was but a moment of contact yet in that instance, where sun, and trees, and quiet greeted me, that my eyes welled up and I let the tears flow. I was in perfect balance and perfectly happy. I was in the moment.

Often we assume that to be fulfilled and happy necessitates a steady diet of grandeur, drama and excitement. In fact, being happy – being in the moment – demands a retreat into oneself to bear what is already there for the taking. Try it. Lose yourself in a favorite activity. Let time stop as you become what you are doing – what you are creating. It will feel great and in that moment, you will be happy.

About the Author

Kita Szpak is a writer, publicist, communications strategist, and speaker whose professional reputation has been built on "positioning clients for excellence" since she opened her consulting business in 1992. Armed with honors degrees in German and Education from Queen's University in Kingston, Canada, as well as business management certification from the Queen's School of Business, Kita cross-pollinates sound business principals with marketing savvy. She has spent over ten years working with prominent Canadian artists, musicians and writers such as Robert Farrell, Maria Knapik, Firdaus Kharas, and Elisabeth Harvor. Last October, Kita published her first children's book, "You're Special Wherever You Are" (www.picturebookstories.com). Last April, Kita also accomplished another first by running the Big Sur International Marathon in California. Her second book, "Tipping Point to Happiness" (www.tippingpointtohappiness. com) with business partner, Monique MacKinnon, made its debut at the

Women Living on the Verge of Evolution Summit and Convocation in Las Vegas in September, 2010.

Wow...I'm Dying
Craig Sim Webb

Since childhood, I have always loved swimming, windsurfing, Scuba diving, rafting, kayaking and canoeing; if it has to do with water sports, you name it and I probably do it and love it. A few months before I turned thirteen, I became the top 200M breaststroke swimmer in Canada for my age group. By fourteen or fifteen, I could swim two lengths of a 25-meter pool underwater without coming up for air. Yet when someone once asked me what I thought the worst way to die was, I answered without hesitation – I most feared death by drowning. It seemed like a strange contradiction, but I guess some things just are not logical, or at least not until we can see a bigger picture.

And so it happened that my new French roommate who guided rafting trips invited me along for a day on Quebec City's nearby Jacques Cartier River. It was fall, and the vibrant red, orange and yellow leaves highlighted against dark green pines smelled wonderful. They swayed in the September breeze under a warm autumn sun that sparkled off the river all around our raft. The water was cool since the rafting season was nearly over. Without a doubt, the Jacques Cartier is a powerful, spectacular river. After a couple hours of white water wildness intermixed with friendly paddling chatter, the growing roar of a large oncoming rapid slowly drowned out our voices. We grew silent and tensed excitedly as the frothing river vortex that was to change my life forever loomed closer. Our boat smacked the churning waters slightly sideways, ramming into the rushing white backflow of a huge souse hole. The raft instantly folded like an upside-down taco and dumped most of it contents, including me. I did not even have time for a breath before I was pulled under. I swirled about in the chilly, dark water. My life vest propelled me toward the surface but my helmet bumped the underside of the boat. I felt a sudden stab of fear. I had no air and could not see which way to go to reach the boat's edge, so I started heading forward, frantically trying to surface again. Unfortunately, I must have been at one end of the raft heading toward the other end lengthwise, since it was near-impossible to see in the swirling water. After frantically trying to pop up for air a few times, everything slowed. I do not remember even feeling the coldness of the water anymore. A single thought washed over my whole awareness, *Wow... I guess this is it – I'm dying.* What was so surprising to me was how the gripping fear suddenly switched to an incredibly deep sense of peace, wonder, and intrigue about the whole situation. I stopped scrambling to get to the surface for a breath. The experience had somehow become strangely very enjoyable. I guess I must have floated and swirled there for a little while. I don't remember exactly what happened after that until somehow I was back in the boat. I guess I eventually popped to the surface and got yanked up by someone on the raft. I don't think my roommate guide ever even asked whether I was okay because she was too busy hauling others back into the boat and trying to steer. Reflecting on the experience later, I began to realize that a subtle yet very profound shift had happened in those moments underwater. I was no longer afraid of drowning, or really very fearful of death for that matter. It was from that point on that very significant changes began to take place.

Many years later, after learning symbolism and developing the Lucid Living framework that I teach for more fully understanding important events, I now see the whole experience not just as a dramatic life moment, but also as a powerful symbolic scenario of sorts that I call a 'waking dream'. That is to say that if one views the situation metaphorically, it is as though I was 'baptized' underwater in a sense, and freed from my fears of drowning and even somewhat of dying.

Traditional views of time might see the psychological and spiritual rebirth that I then started to undergo in my life as perhaps resulting from that event, yet as author Pat Rodegast writes, "Life experiences are the outer symbol of what the soul wants to know." In other words, from a perspective free from linear, sequential *chronos* time, I would say that the waking event I just described was a 'symbolic' enactment in the physical world of a larger, deeper transformation that was already happening within me at other levels. It was the visible tip of my inner catharsis iceberg, so to speak, and a signpost of the beginnings of a much bigger and deeper change. When I shared this perspective with my highly respected colleague Dr. Raymond Moody whose books some of you are surely familiar with, he acknowledged that this was indeed quite a valid way to understand the event. I will even venture to say that my future hopes and dreams for who I could someday become had somehow reached backwards across time, unconsciously guided me to Quebec City, and sparked this momentous and rather grace-filled life transition. I feel much freer and fuller these days, and that awakening event became a key doorway in my past through which my present reality and fullness of life first really became possible.

Shortly after my powerful 'submersion' experience, school break began and I suddenly started remembering up to ten (!) dreams a day. Yes, sometimes ten or more – and many of them often well past lunch and even into following days. This shocked and amazed me, yet I was very curious, so like a good little scientist, I started logging these dreams in a notebook to see what might emerge from it all. Within a week of starting the notebook, I tried a mental technique one night that I had previously developed on my own for reminding myself of things, and I underwent the most incredible experience. I later learned that it was called a lucid (i.e. conscious) dream. I knew during the dream that 'I' was dreaming, while my physical body continued to sleep soundly in bed. The experience did not last long, but it truly astounded me, and made me realize that physical life is really just one station on a larger dial of experience. In the weeks and months after that, more lucid dreams and many other unusual perceptions and other mind-blowing experiences followed that were shocking, very intriguing, and mostly way outside of everything I knew at that time. These experiences radically and quite abruptly transformed and expanded my whole view of the world, of life, and of who "I" am.

To make a long and quite adventurous story short, I spent the years since then exploring various aspects of life that my traditional education did not train me in. I volunteered at Montreal's suicide action hotline and learned how to avoid reacting to stressful emotional situations. Sometimes I would get repeat 'troublemaker' callers to laugh at jokes rather than getting caught in their anger or being led along by their false stories. A couple times at least I was able to get emergency help for people in the middle of a suicide attempt who may have otherwise lost their lives. At 25, I traveled to Ecuador for 6 months to work as a third world development volunteer, and I discovered from an outside perspective what our culture is like – and it was quite an eye-opener! For my education, I finished my physics degree and also continued to integrate my inner explorations with dreams into a more comprehensive view of objective and subjective science. I also had the great blessing to have three guidance dreams that encouraged me to learn non-violent communication, and I am very thankful that I followed them. That communications training, which I studied closely for 7 years, has been such a blessing. It has not only immeasurably helped my personal and professional relationships, but the core perspective that it offers has also allowed me to be much more present and peaceful in tough emotional scenarios because it allows me to always see the true, beautiful intentions behind everyone's actions and know without a doubt that we are all essentially good at heart, though occasionally stuck with rather poor strategies for trying to meet our needs. Another mind-body healing and optimal performance modality I have trained since college that helps a great deal with presence and mindfulness is biofeedback.

Specialized equipment that monitors breathing, heart rate, brainwaves, hand temperature and other physiological measures has permitted myself and clients to physiologically train skills such as focused attention, quiet mind, creativity, deep peace and presence, and much more. For example, one very simple mindfulness technique anyone can use when stressful moments occur is to breathe deeply from the diaphragm six times per minute. This breathing frequency actually affects the heart in a very unique manner that helps to bring about mind-body harmony and a more centered perspective.

I realized early on that nobody else was really going to make my life the amazing adventure I hoped it could be, so I decided I would not sit on the sidelines waiting. Many times I have felt lost, or been immobilized by fear. That I broke through these darker moments is often because I took initiative and moved forward 'anyway', pep-talking myself into finding creative ways to surmount difficult obstacles and empathizing with myself after major disappointments so that I could find the perseverance to pick myself up and continue. Yet I must also acknowledge that there are far too many times to count where I have been supported by friends, family, or by other forms of the amazing grace that has so often helped me through. What has really been most valuable is to have the "inner GPS" guidance that my dreams offer me every day as to what choices and projects will be the most fulfilling, how to navigate relationship challenges as well as possible, and essentially how to love myself as deeply as I now do, even with all my personal peculiarities and continuing challenges. I have so much still to learn, but the inner dream/intuition compass has helped immeasurably to heal serious digestion troubles naturally, resolve painful relationship conflicts, write new songs, make very lucrative business decisions, and advance organically along my path of personal evolution. I am very grateful to now be fortunate enough to enjoy the role of training both individuals and companies how to take more advantage of all the processes I have mentioned to improve health, peace of mind, team synergy, and personal and professional success, and also to be a performing/recording artist and corporate edutainer.

About the Author

Craig Sim Webb is a widely-traveled Speaker/Trainer/Author in applied psychology, communications, and optimal performance. He is an invited expert for Fortune 500 corporations, major motion pictures, and over a thousand international TV/radio/print/online media, and has had the privilege to empower CEOs, celebrities, best-selling Authors, doctors, professors, and many others, helping them make major breakthroughs while having plenty of fun. To learn about online teleclasses, outdoor adventure workshops, and private counseling or corporate training, visit: www. edutainer.ca or www.craigwebb.ca.

Freedom Right Now
Shelley Terracino

In this moment, all is possible. We are limitless, to bring forth any circumstance with one given thought. Here now, is truly precious. Anything can be created, from love. Importance lies behind staying centered. This is where dreams are born. Past 'nows' have transformed from that cause to this effect. Be thankful for this. There is no recreating what has already past. In this deep center space within us connects us to every living thing. Every human, sealion, raindrop and flower. Here now we can feel our truth, wisdom, light, energy and love. In this moment, we are free. Power is held in this moment. Our universal power. Connectedness. There is no other place I would rather be, than in my heart here feeling so free.

About the Author
Shelley was born and raised in Northeastern Pa. Growing up in the country she developed a love for the peaceful, cricket singing natural world. She is currently attending The Institute of Integrative Nutrition based in NYC to become a holistic health counselor. Shes looking forward to her future of helping the community and the world to save them selves, one fruit and vegetable at a time.

Afterword

Thank you so much for spending your precious time reading this book. I was so lucky to have so many incredible contributors and such inspiring essays. After reading these touching essays I was overwhelmed with inspiration and truly felt within my being that this book needed to reach a worldwide audience. I am humbled by being chosen to share this with you and I ask you to share this book with everyone you know so we can all have the ability to live fulfilling lives in this very moment. *Now* is the time to change our lives in order to help change humanity.

Other Books by Richard Singer

Your Daily Walk with the Great Minds
Eastern Wisdom for Your Soul
Daddy, What is Success? with Helen Thomas, and Joseph Betty
Unintelligent Humans…

About the Author

Richard Singer is first of all a real human being who is quite faulty and still struggles with life on a daily basis, however on a worldly basis he is an award winning author, trained psychotherapist, college instructor, and most importantly a seeker of truth. He continuously searches for wisdom to use in his life, as well as helping other human beings in their precious journey. He has studied Eastern Psychology, Buddhist Healing, and Non-Violence at the Doctoral Level; in addition, he has spent years devoted to the study of wisdom recorded throughout history. He seeks to impart this knowledge to the world through his writing. His primary purpose is to benefit humanity in any way possible. Richard states that "My books are not only for reading; they are meant to be lived."

You can find out more about Richard and his books at www. EmbracingthePresent.com or contact him directly at RAS9999@aol. com.

BOOKS

O is a symbol of the world, of oneness and unity. In different cultures it also means the "eye," symbolizing knowledge and insight. We aim to publish books that are accessible, constructive and that challenge accepted opinion, both that of academia and the "moral majority."

Our books are available in all good English language bookstores worldwide. If you don't see the book on the shelves ask the bookstore to order it for you, quoting the ISBN number and title. Alternatively you can order online (all major online retail sites carry our titles) or contact the distributor in the relevant country, listed on the copyright page.

See our website www.o-books.net for a full list of over 500 titles, growing by 100 a year.

And tune in to myspiritradio.com for our book review radio show, hosted by June-Elleni Laine, where you can listen to the authors discussing their books.

MySpiritRadio